RADICAL SURGERY

Reconstructing the American Health Care System

By

Mel Hawkins

ISBN: 1-4033-0625-7

This book is printed on acid free paper.

1st Books - rev. 05/13/02

TABLE OF CONTENTS

FOREWORD

The plight of a rather large number of Americans without health insurance has been recognized for quite some time. Also, over the years, different proposals have been put forth for creating "universal access" to health care services. But, as most people know, the idea of having a national health care program has not found acceptance with the majority of Americans. This may be ironic because almost all Americans, at least in principle, favor some mechanism that would enable everyone to receive health care whenever needed. One of the main points of apprehension generally revolves around the government gaining more control over the financing and delivery of health care.

In this book, Mel Hawkins resurrects the problem faced by many Americans who do not have health insurance. Whereas most of the previous works of this nature have been written from a policy perspective, this book is intended to speak directly to the American consumer with the objective of bringing about a radical change in the current health care delivery system.

The author presents a conceptual model based on the premise that both fee-for-service and managed care systems have been at odds with the interests of the patient. He proposes instead an elimination of the health insurance function carried out by insurance companies and managed care organizations. He also proposes dismantling the current employer-based health insurance system, and elimination of the Medicare and Medicaid programs along with dissolution of the federal agency, Centers for Medicare and Medicaid Services (formerly, Health Care Financing Administration). He believes that elimination of these agencies will save enough money to extend health insurance to those who currently have no coverage. The author proposes replacing the current structures with a federal tax that will be distributed by the federal government to community-based primary care physicians throughout the country. These physicians will be responsible for providing primary care and for purchasing specialized services, including hospital-based care, on behalf of their patients.

Like all other proposals calling for a complete overhaul of health care, proposals in this book are also subject to debate and controversy.

In *Radical Surgery*, the author makes a meaningful contribution to this debate over the future of the American health care system and the author's appeal to consumers puts them in the best position to debate the merits of the proposed reforms.

Douglas A. Singh, Ph.D., M.B.A.
Associate Professor
School of Public and Environmental Affairs
Indiana University-South Bend.

Co-author: Shi, Leiyu and Douglas A. Singh, *Delivering Health Care in America: A Systems Approach*, 2nd Edition, Aspen Publishers, Gaithersburg, MD, 2001.

PREFACE & ACKNOWLEDGEMENTS

My intent from the beginning of this project was to write a book for a general audience. The issue of health care affects us all and it is my conviction that any solution to the health care dilemma in our great nation must involve all American men and women.

The list of academic and professional books, articles and essays on the subject of health care and health care reform is vast, yet few of these works have come to the attention of the populace. In an effort to keep this book off of that auspicious list, I have tried to present the issues of health care in the broadest of strokes. I also wanted to avoid the need for the in-depth documentation so important to the academic and professional world, but so tedious and alien to the general reader. Although the solution I have offered is, I believe, original, the overwhelming body of material utilized to lay the foundation for these ideas has become common knowledge.

For the reader who is intrigued by the subject of health care and thirsts for more detail, the bibliography offers a number of works that would be worth the reader's time and investment. My recommendation would be to begin with the book by Leiyu Shi and Doug Singh, *Delivering Health Care in America: A Systems Approach*. This book provides a comprehensive look at our health care system and the issues that confront it and also offers a virtual library of resource material.

My sincere thanks to the many friends and family members whose assistance and support has been invaluable. I am indebted to Professor Doug Singh for his advice and guidance. I would also like to thank those friends and family members who helped with the arduous process of proof reading. This list includes my father; my daughter Jeanne and my good friend Janet Langley. I also appreciate the help of Roy Wilson at Parkview Hospital and his young associate who directed me to recent research that proved especially useful. A special thanks to my good friends Mike Peters and Bill Badie, whose help and support has been incredible. A mention, also, of my new friends in the beanblossom writers' group whose commitment to providing support and encouragement to one another is inspiring. Of course, a thank you to my son, Eric, and my daughters, Jeanne and Laura for their love and encouragement. And, last but not least, to my beautiful wife and best friend, Chris, my greatest source of joy.

INTRODUCTION

The attempt to understand the American health care system, in all of its complexity, seems almost overwhelming. The system is like a ship in the midst of a hurricane with powerful forces smashing down on it from every direction. Health care reform has been a topic of debate for decades yet now, in the twenty-first century, it is reported that as many as forty-five million Americans lack adequate health coverage. Many have no coverage at all. Is there another issue affecting so many people and about which so little is being done?

Contrary to conventional wisdom with respect to health care, we can have it all. We can provide universal coverage, equitably to all Americans. We can do it for about what we spend today, possibly less. We can make it simple for both the patient and provider. We can place control over the practice of medicine in the hands of the physician. We can do all of this with minimal involvement on the part of government and we can rely on market forces to drive quality.

During the Nixon presidency, efforts were made to change the way health care was provided with the promotion of the HMO concept and, although Health Maintenance Organizations and other managed care companies prosper today, they have proven controversial and have not lived up to the expectation that they would become the saving grace of health care. Make no mistake; health care has changed as a result of managed care. While there is evidence to suggest that there has been a positive impact on the cost of care, many patients and providers will tell you those changes have resulted in more, rather than fewer problems.

In the seventies and eighties, many reforms were proposed and much legislation passed, but few of these initiatives resulted in more than cosmetic changes. The most significant impact of these reforms, some would argue, has been increased bureaucracy.

At the beginning of the Clinton administration, health care was once again in the forefront, however even Clinton, a President so popular that he survived both scandal and impeachment, lacked the power and determination to bring the issue of health care to any kind of satisfying resolution. Instead we have muddled through another decade having done little more than tinker with a system we do not comprehend and that will not bend to our will. The result, once again, has been more bureaucracy and increased complexity.

We come to an end of a thirty-year period in which the price of health care has more than lapped inflation while the product for which we have so dearly paid is less satisfactory to those who can afford care and less accessible to those who cannot.

As we begin a new century, having endured another presidential campaign, the ritual debate is renewed, but in muted tones. Health care has joined taxes, budget cuts, crime reduction, welfare reform, and world peace as a standard plank without which a candidate cannot possibly be elected, even though the electorate has long learned to expect minimal results.

How is it that health care has been added to this list of noble but improbable causes? Possibly, because we have learned that we cannot purchase health, we are lulled into the notion that universal health care is also beyond our means. It is at this point, by replacing the pessimism of the past with a new optimism, that the journey to high-quality, comprehensive health care for all Americans commences.

Universal health care is one noble cause that is within our reach, but to realize the dream we must alter our approach. The only thing preventing us from caring for every American man, woman and child is our lack of will. Building a system that will meet the needs of our citizens, like travelling to the Moon, may seem so complicated that it appears to be unachievable, but this is only an illusion. We traveled to the Moon because we chose to exercise our will and one day we will travel to Mars propelled by that same indomitable will. Universal health care, at a price we can afford, like manned space flight, is a practical, human-engineering problem with a solution, provided we are willing to apply the same focused, well-resourced, problem-solving approach as did the men and women of NASA.

Quality medical care is ours for the choosing. What we lack is:

- a consensus that all Americans, by virtue of their membership in the human race, deserve competent medical care and treatment;
- a thorough understanding of our present health care delivery system and the forces that drive it;
- A new design engineered to produce the results we seek;
- the willingness to commit the necessary resources, and

- the tenacity to overcome the obstacles in our path, the greatest of which is the power of special interest groups

So many of the health-care-system problems we experience today result from reforms that have not only failed, but never had a chance to succeed because the logical premise upon which they were based was faulty. Understanding must come before reform if we are to have any hope the change will be meaningful and sustainable. Many have worked hard to bring about reform of the system, yet for all of their efforts and best intentions, the changes that were forthcoming were responses to symptomology not fully understood within the context of the system viewed as a whole. Further, these reforms were both driven and influenced by the vested interests of the proponents. It is impossible to underestimate the far-ranging, negative impact these partisan interests have wreaked.

At the beginning of every project or initiative it is a good practice to define one's purpose. Why are we extending this effort and what do we expect to accomplish? In this book our purpose is to challenge the reader to take a fresh look at the American health care delivery system so that we can construct a new system, tailored to our needs. By fresh look we mean with a new perspective. This is not a simple task. Human beings are a repository of biases and preconceptions, all of which color our view of the world. Setting these preconceptions aside is what the reader must do if he or she is to be able to evaluate the efficacy of the health care model we will be proposing in this work.

What we propose is a different approach and one that can easily be mislabeled or misunderstood. We offer a model that will permanently resolve the most critical issues regarding the way medicine is practiced in this country, the way we make care available to our citizens and, finally, the way we pay the cost of this medical care.

The reader will see a radical departure from the system in operation today. Because we use some of the same terminology, however, and even borrow bits and pieces of the existing health care system, readers will be tempted to form premature judgments about this important issue on the basis of their own perspective and their own experiences with the current system. For those with strong biases or who have a vested interest in our existing delivery system, the

3

necessary openness and objectivity will be even more difficult. For some it will be nearly impossible, not because they are unintelligent and unimaginative, but because they examine not so much to understand as to rebut.

The United States is a wonderful country populated by generally well-educated men and women who take their freedoms of belief and expression seriously. American men and women are not always right in what they believe, but they are rarely in doubt. This characteristic of strong advocacy for the things in which one believes is both a blessing and a curse. It is part of the strength of character that helped us build the richest and most powerful nation on Earth, but it is also one of the sources of our weakness as manifested by our prejudices.

We ask our readers to suspend their skepticism and withhold judgment. This issue of health care is too important to our country and its people. Surely we can agree there is something tragic and intolerable about a system of care comprised of the best physicians, the best hospitals, the best ancillary providers, and the best technology in the world, yet leaves so many millions of our brethren on the outside looking in. Surely we can agree that a system so complicated that the average American struggles to comprehend it, is unacceptable. Surely we can agree a system so full of bureaucratic controls that our providers' ability to practice quality medicine is impaired, is a travesty. Surely we can brand as a fiscal failure a system in which so many of our health care dollars are spent on activities that add no value and are not related to the direct care of patients.

We must do something to solve the problems of our health care system. Motivational speaker, Zig Ziglar, in one of his books writes, "If we keep doin' what we've been doin' we'll keep gettin' what we've been gettin'." We can no longer afford to keep pulsing down the same path. Radical change is needed and the only way we will bring about dramatic, meaningful change is to reconstruct our system of care on a new foundation, with a new premise, unburdened by our prejudices, unimpeded by the special interests groups and, focused on our purpose. Health care is clearly an issue in which the only interest group that counts is the American people as a whole.

As you begin the journey through this book, set aside your biases and open your mind to a new idea. Only after you have begun to understand the underlying logic of that which we propose, at its most fundamental level, is it appropriate to begin formulating judgments and taking positions. If at the conclusion of your reading you don't buy the solution, then you have lost nothing and learned something new in the process. If, however, as we believe will be the case, the ideas proposed here begin to click for you, then we will have taken the first critical step toward a new vision in which every American will receive the medical care they require at a price the U.S. can afford to pay.

To accomplish this seemingly improbable objective we must do two things. We must not only alter the way we think about our health care system, we must take the responsibility for bringing about such a radical reconstruction of the health care system out of the hands of the politicians, the policy makers and the political action committees. As powerful as these men and women may be they are constrained by there own vested interests.

A change of this magnitude can only be driven by the most powerful force in the world – the American consumer/taxpayer/voter.

We must also acknowledge that no health care plan can work without the buy-in, or at least the cooperation, of physicians and no group is more suspicious of health care reform. And why shouldn't physicians be suspicious? Every health care reform initiative in the professional lifetime of most doctors in medical practice today has led to more complication, has reduced the amount of control physicians have over their own practices and the quality of care they provide and, finally, has made it more difficult for physicians to collect payment for the work they do.

There is every reason to expect that physicians will be just as suspicious of this proposal for a National Health Care Plan. Before they read this work and take a look at the system that I will propose, I ask them to do four things. I ask them first, to imagine what the future of health care will be if we keep trudging down the same path of incremental reform. Is there any reason to believe the system will get better, become less complicated, provide more freedom to practice quality medicine, or become more lucrative? Is there any reason to believe we will see a return to the unregulated, fee-for-service system that physicians recall with such fondness?

I would also ask physicians to consider that any change that will make the practice of medicine better for the patient and practitioner alike, must be so radical, so revolutionary, that it will bear little

5

similarity to the system now in place. It will take such a proposal to ignite the imagination of the public.

Thirdly, I ask that the physician consider the proposal I am about to make with an open mind. It is a proposal for a system that will place control of health care in the hands of the physician. It is a proposal that will give physicians the freedom to practice medicine without interference from public or private bureaucracies. It is a system that will minimize the money spent on activity that has nothing to do with the direct care of patients and, that will funnel all of the money currently spent on health care to those who provide care to patients. It is a system in which patients will be free to choose their provider and it will be a system where the role of government is limited to the very few things governments do well.

Finally, I would ask physicians to resist the natural inclination to conclude that a system as radical as that which I propose is problematic, that it cannot be implemented. In the last chapter of this book I lay out a simple but powerful plan that will bring the enormous power of the American consumer into play to work toward implementation of this proposal. As physicians review this implementation plan I ask them to consider the powerful impact that they, working together with their patients, could have on the political process we will describe.

Imagine for just a moment the impact if, say, just one quarter of all primary care physicians would encourage their patients to take the action steps discussed. I predict that, if this were to happen, the health plan I am proposing could become a reality in as little as two years.

Sound preposterous? Maybe, maybe not. Remember that one cannot find a cure for a problem as complicated as health care until one takes the time to examine a new idea. Health care is a compelling issue as the health of millions of Americans is at stake. Whether we can find the will to breathe life into this vision is entirely up to you, the reader.

SECTION I
SETTING THE STAGE

What is our purpose? How did health care get to where it is today? How does health care fail and what are the root causes of that failure? Where do we begin the process of solving the problems of health care and meeting the needs of the American people?

Mel Hawkins

A young woman in Indiana, twenty-eight years of age, seemed poised for a good life. She liked her job in a small professional office where she was respected for her consistent performance. She enjoyed the people with whom she worked and she was engaged to be married, in only a few months, to a young man with whom she was thoroughly in love. Life was happy, busy and could hardly have been better so she paid little attention when she experienced occasional dizziness and a slight numbness in her left arm and leg. These symptoms were followed by blurred vision and headaches and at the urging of her family and her fiancée she went to her doctor.

Although she had no health insurance – her employer was a small business and offered no benefits – her physician was able to arrange for a stream of increasingly more sophisticated and more expensive diagnostic procedures and, a referral to a neurologist. The diagnosis was Multiple Sclerosis. By this time the young woman's symptoms had progressed and her physician pronounced her disabled and unable to work. Reluctantly she quit her job – at that time she truly was unable to perform her duties – and applied to Social Security for a disability.

After a lengthy process, during which her symptoms began to abate, the application for disability was rejected by Social Security. Although she felt much better, and was able to return to work, she was told that the MS symptoms might recur and could be even more debilitating. She was now a twenty-nine year old woman whose life was not so promising. She was unemployed, thousands of dollars in debt, and lived with the fear her health could deteriorate at any time. Her fiancée had stuck by her during the ordeal but the couple was advised to postpone their wedding, as a husband would become liable for her indebtedness. Heartbroken, frightened, discouraged and deeply in debt, she filed for bankruptcy.

Eventually she found a new job – her previous one no longer available – and although she didn't care for the work or co-workers nearly as well as her prior job, a group health plan was offered. Unfortunately her MS was ruled as a pre-existing condition that would not be covered, at least during the first year. The monthly payroll deduction for the health insurance premium reduced her take home pay by twenty percent.

This young woman had become a victim, not only of her illness, but also of the system. The health care providers who took the

8

financial risk to provide care for this patient were left with little choice but to write off a portion of the charges for their service. Although not visible to the public, costs such as these must be born by the system and they fuel the fires of medical inflation. There is no such thing as a free service, and someone, somewhere must pay.

CHAPTER 1

WHAT IS OUR PURPOSE?

Why the concerns about health care? Certainly not because we have bad physicians, substandard hospitals, poorly trained nurses and other ancillary personnel and not because the technology of health care in the United States is outdated. Although there are many issues on which we disagree the facts are undisputed. Health care costs are out of control and, in spite of the high price we pay for health care, the needs of millions of Americans go unattended.

Approximately fifteen percent of the American people live with inadequate health coverage and the group widens with each wave of new births and new immigrations, the latter whether legal or not. For those who have health insurance protection there are still problems and numerous sources of disenchantment. The cost of care rises incessantly and the process of obtaining the care we require grows more complicated with each step. We are not even free, in many instances, to choose our providers. Additionally, for those of us covered by an employer-sponsored health plan, at least once per year we live with the knowledge that our employer may choose a different carrier, one that requires us to change providers. Whomever our provider, we increasingly find ourselves disappointed in the amount of attention our physicians are willing and/or able to offer.

Notwithstanding an assembly line of reforms proposed and implemented by some of the best minds of the twentieth century, the health care system still fails to meet the needs and expectations of the nation. Most, if not all of the reforms of the last half-century have resulted in more complexity and more bureaucracy than the system they were intended to remedy, causing even more restricted access and higher costs. Is there any reason to think new reforms will be any less disappointing? If our attempts to repair the existing system seem destined for failure, what is the answer?

Do we accept things as they are and make the best of them? Or, do we replicate the health care systems of other countries in the western world, with the Canadian system a prime example. There is no question the Canadian system works, as do others in Europe. In Canada virtually every citizen has unobstructed access to care at no charge and, the cost to the Canadian people has not been unreasonable.

In an article in the *Los Angeles Times*, John-Thor Dahlburg and Richard Boudreaux write:

> "... *Europe gives the ordinary citizen an enormous sense of security. In many countries, people never have to worry about being deprived of essential health services – or prescription drugs ... because they can't afford them.*"

Dahlburg and Boudreaux also cite a 191-country survey by the World Health Organization that states:

> "*The United States – which lays out a bigger share of its income on health than any other country, at 14 percent of all generated wealth – ranked 37th ... barely edging out No. 39 Cuba*" (*Los Angeles Times*, November 2, 2000).

Yet, even if we were to admit the Canadian system and those of other countries would work, there is something alien about these approaches in the minds of many Americans.

Americans, it seems, like things American. History is replete with examples of American resistance to foreign solutions. Give that foreign alternative even the slightest resemblance to socialism or, worse yet, communism and you can forget about it. Pride in American accomplishment and emblazoned memories of the failures and the mediocre results of socialist ideas and government-run programs run deep in the psyche of the American people. We accept foreign consumer products, begrudgingly if we're honest about it, only because their quality is good and because their products are the output of a capitalist economy. Capitalism is, after all, at least in the minds of Americans, an American invention other nations have only borrowed.

What we require is a health care system that is uniquely American, designed by Americans and operated by American citizens, not government. Americans want a system that looks, feels and smells American. We are a nation of innovators and inventors, of hard working men and women who, if not entrepreneurial, have at least been touched at some time and in some way by the entrepreneurial spirit. It is part of our American heritage. We are also a people who believe we can do almost anything. If it can be imagined, it can be realized. So, if the system we have today will not work to our satisfaction and we find foreign systems objectionable, the only course left to us, other than living with an unsatisfactory situation, is to invent a system tailored to our needs and expectations.

It is the thesis of this work that an American system that meets the needs of all Americans is well within our capability and also within our means.

To achieve this objective we must take the time to understand what it is we need from a health care delivery system and we must go back to the drawing board and build it. It is vital, however, that we start with a blank spreadsheet. If we have learned anything from our efforts at health care reform it is that we pay an unacceptable price for our reliance on patchwork remedies and fixes.

We will start with a process that takes us logically from where we are today to solid ground on which to build this new American model. Our objective is an understanding. To learn rather than validate our own assumptions and biases. Why does our system fail and what contributes to that failure? Our purpose is not to be critical or to look for evil intent on the part of the actors in the system. Anyone can be critical and we know well how much is accomplished with criticism.

Our first step will be the establishment of a set of ground rules. They are simple rules but critical to the success of our venture.

The first rule calls for readers to set aside their biases and preconceptions, to challenge their assumptions and avoid a rush to judgment. We need to think creatively, outside the box, unencumbered by negative thoughts or by concerns about practicability. Such distractions will not serve our purpose.

The second rule is to begin with the objective in mind. We must start with a clear definition of goal and purpose and, periodically, we need to pause and recalibrate lest we wander off our heading.

Rule three is to operate on the premise that the interests of the few must be set aside in favor of the interests of the whole. We must be prepared to resist the influence of special interest groups, no matter how rich and powerful, with our focus on the only interest group that matters, the American people.

Rule number four is that we must put perfection out of our mind. There are no perfect solutions to human problems, health care included.

Fifth is to forget about exceptions. There will always be exceptions to the rule but we cannot design a logical system on the basis of exceptions. A good system will be adaptable and able to accommodate both the extraordinary and the peculiar.

The sixth and final rule is to remember that anything man can imagine, man can do. We must let our imagination and creativity run free. The greatest obstacles to our success reside in our own minds.

Objectives and Expected Outcomes

Our purpose is simply to devise a health care system that meets our needs and expectations, nothing more and nothing less. We begin like a design engineer faced with a tool that fails to produce the desired results. His job, to build a tool that performs to our expectations and specifications.

What is it that we want from our health care delivery system?

The first thing we want is a system that is fully accessible. By this we mean there are no barriers to keep American men, women and children from the medical care they require to live a full and productive life to the limits of their talents and capabilities. Affluence must have no influence. Race, sex, age, religion, ethnicity, language, sexual preference or any other artificial criteria must be given zero consideration. The only qualification necessary is membership in the American family. Neither can access be limited for geographical reasons. Within reasonable limits access must be assured for people living in rural, urban or suburban communities alike.

Secondly, our health care system must be affordable and, if at all possible, we want to reduce aggregate U.S. health care expenses. We derive no pleasure or utility from a luxury car we cannot afford to own. By affordable we do not mean cheap. We want the best value money can buy as measured by both effectiveness and efficiency. Money spent on activity unrelated to providing or supporting direct care to patients must be minimized and the cost of care must not be so high we are unable to provide for other vital needs of our society, whether national defense, justice, education or cultural enrichment. These things are essential to the health and well being of people and a nation. Neither can health care languish in favor of other necessities. Quality health care is also an indispensable component of a civilized nation. That such care is unavailable to so many of our brethren is a chink in our national armor. It weakens us as a nation and places our future at risk.

Another essential ingredient for our health care system is excellence. We want the best providers, the best facilities, the best technology, the best medicines, and the best knowledge in the world. We believe these assets are in place today and we are unwilling to settle for anything less. Second best is unacceptable, as is mediocrity.

Quality health care doesn't just happen. It is no different than quality in any other enterprise in which a product or service is produced. Market forces drive quality. If we want quality we must be willing and able to make an investment in our critical assets. Investments must be made in recruiting and retaining the best people and we must also invest in their ongoing training and development as professionals. Further investments are essential if these talented people are to have high quality resources at their disposal. How else can they assure us of a high return on our investment. In a free market system it is the quality of our product or service that will determine the extent to which our investments will earn an acceptable return.

Crucial to quality is our willingness to place our trust in the talents, skills, wisdom and professionalism of our health care professionals. Talented people must be given the freedom and latitude to learn, grow and to challenge ideas, albeit in the context of accountability. What is more characteristic of an American system than an individual's freedom to develop and apply his abilities with minimal barriers and interference? This must also be part of the character of the American health care delivery system.

Finally, we want equity. If one segment of our society has access to a high quality of care and another segment has access only to a lower quality of care, the gap between the "haves" and the "have nots" can only widen and this serves the interests of neither the individual nor the whole.

These ingredients can be combined to produce our ideal health care system and they also define our mission in this venture. There are numerous other issues about which we will be concerned, but each of them will be defined within the context of these most fundamental requirements.

We must also recall whom we exist to serve. Clearly the answer is the American people. We do not exist to serve special interest groups whether the American Medical Association, the American Hospital Association, the managed care industry or the health insurance industry. Neither do we strive to oppose or harm these groups. When the interests of these groups do not parallel the interests of the people as a whole, however, we will entertain no thoughts of compromise.

It is prudent, at this juncture, to recall our commitment to set aside questions of practicability. Let's not be diverted by individual judgments about what is realistic and what is not. Nothing we possess today would have been considered realistic by our parents even fifty years ago. Such negativism can only dilute the power and the magic of the human imagination and of American ingenuity, and this cannot be permitted.

Where Do We Begin

Our first task is to identify, in broad strokes, the deficiencies of the U.S. health care system. Once we have identified those aspects of our system with which we are dissatisfied we can begin our examination of the system as a whole. The search is for root causes or, if one prefers to think in medical terms, the underlying pathology. This is a crucial stage of the process. It is so easy for human beings to jump to premature conclusions or rush to judgment. Interestingly enough, this propensity results from the way the human brain functions. A remarkable instrument, the brain works ceaselessly to make sense out of the stimuli flying at us from every vector, in all dimensions of the environment. The more familiar the brain becomes with certain stimuli, the more likely it is to begin to label that stimuli, then take it for granted. If it did not categorize information our brains would simply be overwhelmed by the complexity of the universe.

Our challenge is to maintain an awareness of this learning process lest we be fooled by superficial evidence and mistake symptoms for causal factors and forces. If we are not diligent in this effort we will fail to recognize the forces of change and never realize the thing we think we understand is not at all what we believe it to be.

We will address this so prevalent human tendency by using a process called systems thinking. A systems-thinking approach helps us maintain our diligence and facilitates our journey to an orbital vantagepoint from which health care is visible as a whole. *"Systems thinking is a conceptual framework, a body of knowledge and tools that have been developed over the past fifty years, to make the full patterns clearer, and to help us see how to change them effectively."* (Senge, 1990)

To understand a system, any system, one must consider the whole. In *The Fifth Discipline*, Peter Senge writes:

> *"Business and other human endeavors are also systems. They, too, are bound by an invisible fabric of interrelated actions that often take years for their impact on each other to fully play out. Since we are part of the lacework ourselves, it's doubly hard to see the whole pattern of change. Instead, we tend to focus on snapshots of isolated parts of the system, and wonder why our deepest problems never seem to get solved.*
>
> *"... systems thinking makes understandable the subtlest aspect of the learning organization – the new way individuals perceive themselves and their world. At the heart of the learning organization is a shift of mind – from seeing ourselves as separate from the world to connected to the world, from seeing problems as caused by someone or something "out there" to seeing how our actions create the problems we experience. A learning organization is a place where people are continually discovering how they create their reality. And how they can change it."*

Health care provides a marvelous example of a system not recognized or evaluated as a "whole." Over the years the complexity of health care has grown exponentially and the more complex it becomes the more obscure the underlying logic. Each person has a mental model of the medical services' field and for many this mental model has entrapped us.

An individual might, for example, believe health care costs are out of control as a result of the greed of both providers and insurers, all of whom are more concerned about profits than about the health of their patients. A person with this mental model may well advocate the implementation of more stringent controls, checks and balances.

Ironically these critics, like the rest of us, when confronted with an illness, demand the most comprehensive care available because, after all, their insurance will pay for it. These same men and women have their attorney on standby in the event of a litigious opportunity. These critics react to symptoms rather than focus on the system as a whole. Neither do these men and women see the impact their own actions have on the system. From their vantagepoint the causes of the system's problems are external.

An insurance executive may believe practitioners should be their partner in the battle to manage costs, but they possess a mental model that views medical practitioners as more concerned with generating revenue and minimizing their liability than practicing the kind of medicine that is in the best interests of the patients and the payers. Concerned about the manner in which this perceived attitude impacts on their costs, driving premium rates to new highs while shrinking profits, the insurance executive advocates more controls, more narrow eligibility, more pre-certifications, and more restrictions on the manner in which procedures are coded. The adverse consequences of these strategies are too far removed in time to allow the insurance professional visibility of the ripples that radiate from his actions. These players envision themselves as fiscal guardians of the health care system and have no insight into the role they play in the burgeoning bureaucracy of health care or, in the escalation of health care costs. From their perspective the forces driving these problems are external.

Medical practitioners may have a mental model in which government regulation and insurer red tape are making it increasingly difficult to practice the kind and quality of medicine which drew them to choose a career in medicine. These providers may, at the macro level, fight government interference or increased insurance complexity while, at the micro level, they experiment with new billing or coding strategies in order to optimize reimbursement. These practitioners have reacted to the symptoms and will not recognize the role their actions play in the escalation of the complexity and regulations. Their mental model is etched in granite and they have become their jobs. They perceive the cause of the dilemma to be external, with both the patient and the practitioner among the victims.

Another advocate for the welfare of the people may operate from a mental model that views health care as an entitlement. These men and women are spurred to action by the growing number of people who either have no access to care or who receive care that is inadequate with respect to their needs. These individuals lobby for expanded governmental health programs for those with limited access to care or, at the extreme, for some form of national health care plan. These well-meaning men and women do not recognize the extent to which the programs implemented by government, in a genuine attempt to respond to their concerns, contribute to the complexity of the system and trigger unanticipated consequences. Again, too much time elapses and there is too much complexity for these individuals to recognize how the actions flowing from their mental model have contributed to the problem. They see themselves in the noble role of leader in a battle with a myriad of external forces in conflict with their own vision.

If we look back over the past several decades at the escalation of regulation and the complexity of health care offerings, we can begin to see the system as a whole. Health care has become a latticework of quick fixes and artfully conceived incremental initiatives. As a result, in a period of unprecedented prosperity, our nation spends more than $1.2 trillion per year on health care, yet fails to meet the needs of the whole population.

Systems thinking provides a vehicle which facilitates our examination and makes it easier to understand health care as a whole, but it requires those involved in this process to alter their mental models.

In his book, *The 7 Habits of Highly Effective People*, Steven Covey talks about a paradigm shift after which we begin to see the world from a new perspective. As we approach the task of not only making sense out of the health care system in the United States, but also irrevocably altering it, we must experience this "shift of mind" or "paradigm shift."

If we continue to think about health care in its present context it is as if we are trying to view the planet Earth from our back yard. The entire planet is simply not visible from there. We see the Earth around us and begin to draw inferences and make assumptions on the basis of the information we process through our sensory organs. To an extent our inferences are valid, but the reality is so much broader and more complex. And, the system is powered by forces imperceptible to us from where we sit. We catch glimpses of these forces but they influence the system in ways we cannot see and do not fully understand. The adage "a little bit of knowledge is a dangerous thing" speaks with fluency. Is it any wonder our conclusions are so often off the mark and our actions so unproductive?

Early physicians did their best to treat the infirmities of man using the collective wisdom of their age, totally unaware of the impact bacteria and viruses have on living organisms. The models constructed by the physicians of this period were logical and true to the premise on which they were founded. It was upon this logic that their rationale for action was conceived and they practiced their craft oblivious to their fallacy.

When the role bacteria and viruses play in the etiology of disease was revealed, the whole world of medicine was beamed to a new paradigm and the treatment protocols of the previous model were discarded, no longer relevant.

Today we find ourselves at a similar point in the evolving history of health care and we need another shift of mind. Once we begin to view health care as a logical construct of this new perspective, we can begin to focus our attention on the true root causes of the problems facing health care in the United States. By focusing on root causes, undistracted by mere symptoms, a new set of solutions will surface and we can begin moving into a new reality. We will have experienced a transformation and none too soon.

An eighty-year old woman's foot pain prompted a trip to a podiatrist and after a brief examination she was told she had bone spurs on her heel. Until recently the patient had been remarkably healthy but it seemed that her health had begun to diminish. Her podiatrist explained that there were two treatment alternatives for her to consider, one invasive and the other not. Concerned about the overall welfare of his elderly patient the podiatrist recommended orthotics as the preferred choice, rather than surgery.

Under normal circumstances surgery offered a high probability of success, possibly bringing her permanent relief but it also posed a very real risk that the trauma of the surgery might have adverse consequences. The podiatrist had received good results from the application of orthotics in cases of this type. While not correcting the condition there was a reasonable chance that this solution would give her significant relief from the pain with minimal risk, if any at all. Although not inexpensive, the cost of orthotics was much less than the cost of surgery. Not insignificantly, the orthotics generated less revenue for the podiatry practice. The final advantage, the podiatrist explained, is that if the orthotics produce disappointing results, surgery remains an option.

The patient and her family agreed to move forward with the orthotics. An inquiry to Medicare and to the supplemental carrier revealed, however, that orthotics were not covered and the patient would bear the full cost of the treatment. The surgery, on the other hand, would be fully covered. The patient, a frail woman on a fixed income, must now choose between the treatment she prefers, but that will pose a financial hardship and the surgery that she dreads, but which will be covered. That surgery results in much greater cost to the system only adds to the irony.

This is only one of countless examples where treatment decisions of providers in all venues are influenced and often driven by the interests of third parties, rather than by the interests of the patient. Understand that this was not the intent of the system. In every case the decisions that led to the insurance, Medicare or Medicaid rules that regulate these activities, were implemented with a belief that they would protect rather than harm patients.

CHAPTER 2

HEALTH CARE IN THE US, PAST AND PRESENT

The most critical problems with our current system of health care delivery are relatively easy to identify as we experience them daily.

- Between forty and fifty million people lack adequate coverage
- Costs are rising at a rate faster than the consumer price index
- As many as forty percent of U. S. bankruptcies result from large medical bills
- Increasing complexity of the health insurance and managed care environment for both patient and provider
- Diminishing proportion of primary care practitioners to the whole physician population and the corresponding increase in the number of new physicians who choose a sub-specialty

The Early Years

Before we can find a solution we must understand how these deficiencies have evolved and this requires a brief excursion into the history of health care in the United States. To comprehend why numerous efforts to modify the existing system are viewed as failures, we must review how the fee-for-service system, the role of the private insurance industry, and the role of government have evolved to present form.

In the developing years the physician, usually working alone, delivered care out of the office, in the patient's home or in the hospital and he (and more often than not the early physician was male) accepted payment in cash, trade or barter. The physician was part of the community; everyone knew him and he knew everybody. He had a stake in the health and welfare of the community and its people. Because most people could make some type of payment, doctors of this period were flexible. As a result most Americans who lived in areas within reasonable proximity of a physician's office could generally be assured of access to basic care. The system worked remarkably well as long as the patient's needs were basic and, could be handled out of the local doc's little black bag.

If the patient's problems were complicated and required either the input of a specialist or hospitalization, access became a little more difficult. Specialists were relatively few in number, tended to be centered in large population centers and, they almost always required cash payment for services; the latter, not because the specialist was cold-hearted, but because he probably did not know or have a relationship with the patient. Often the specialist and patient were not part of the same community.

Whether or not a hospital would accept charity cases was usually determined by its charter and/or its location. The not-for-profit hospitals, many of which were church affiliated, typically had as part of its charter a commitment to provide charity care. In larger cities where there was a significant affluent population one might find private hospitals. It would be uncommon for such a facility to handle charity cases. In communities where the "charity" hospitals were absent or overcrowded, many people of modest or limited means went without treatment.

The Advent of Health Insurance

Other than isolated forays by certain industries or communities in the 19th century, it was not until the Great Depression of the 1930's that the concept of health insurance on any sizeable scale emerged. The first significant initiative came from hospitals in several large cities in the form of hospitalization coverage. This "birth of the Blues," as it were, spread in the early thirties, culminating in 1934, with the endorsement of the Blue Cross Plan by the American Hospital Association. Blue Cross was a not-for-profit plan offering comprehensive hospital coverage for its enrollees.

It was another dozen years before similar coverage was available for the medical portion of health care costs. Blue Shield, a not-for-profit plan to cover physician charges, was endorsed by the American Medical Association in 1946.

The Blue Cross and Blue Shield plans were straightforward, with payment for covered services on behalf of enrollees made directly to providers. These "service plans" were available in the years following World War II, for those who could afford to purchase the coverage.

   Capitalizing on the opportunities demonstrated by the Blues, the private insurance industry, already marketing pension and disability coverage, entered the health insurance marketplace on a for-profit basis. Because of their ability to be flexible and responsive, they quickly garnered a share of the health insurance market.

   While the coverage available from the Blues was excellent, health care costs were on the rise, driving premiums upward, and the privates were able to compete effectively on price. The Blues, committed as they were to comprehensive "service" coverage (meaning the policy covered all of the costs of care) and their use of community rates (establishing one premium rate for a whole community) could only pass their swelling costs on to the customer in the form of higher premiums. Enter the private, for-profit plans, with their innovative approaches and the marketplace changed. Their strategies, "indemnity coverage" and variable "experience rating" enabled them to compete effectively on price.

   [Note: Some Americans, even today, are confused by the term "not-for-profit," thinking such organizations exist only to provide a service and need not make money. A not-for-profit agency, regardless of the altruism of its mission, must still be an economically viable entity. A not-for-profit entity must generate sufficient revenue to cover its cost of doing business, but it must also generate surplus revenues (another word for profits) to reinvest in its growth and development. Like their for-profit counterparts, these agencies still have payrolls to meet and trade payables to pay, as well. The primary functional distinction between the for-profits and the not-for-profits is that the latter must reinvest in its mission while in the former the profits are also reinvested, but a portion must accrue to the stockholders.]

   Indemnity coverage, indemnifying or protecting the purchaser against specific risks, allowed great flexibility in offering tailored coverage schemes at a price more favorable than that offered by the Blues. For example, coverage might not commence until the insured had paid out the first $500, at which time the plan would then share the cost of the care with the insured. We know these as deductibles and copays and they were then, and still are an effective strategy. The public's greatest fears are 1) not being able to afford an expensive procedure needed by a member of the family and 2) being wiped out financially by a catastrophic illness. As we have already noted, a significant proportion of bankruptcies in the U.S. result from medical expenses. These factors, coupled with an American propensity to gamble that as long as one is protected from the worst-case scenario he or she might not require any services, provides the insured with the chance to save the difference in premium costs between the lower priced indemnity plan and the higher priced service plan.

This phenomenon also contributed significantly to the overall cost of medical care. Prices in any market will inevitably rise, assuming there is demand for the product or service, unless one of two things happen. The first is competition, which effectively changes the equilibrium between the forces of supply and demand, and the second is regulation. Initially there was little if any governmental regulation and the Blues plans did not behave as if there was competition from the private insurer, whether they recognized it or not. And, as long as the Blues' pricing was driven upward by cost pressures, there was no incentive for the privates to restrain prices. Later, additional insurers joined the game and the Blues adapted by offering alternative coverage packages comparable to what the privates offered.

In the interim, the Blues' plans experienced significant adverse selection much as the HMO's would do in more recent years. Individuals or groups that could anticipate the need for more care, paid a little extra up front for the more comprehensive coverage. It was a simple logic, pay a little more now to avoid higher costs at a later time.

As it turns out, even if the Blue Cross and Blue Shield plans had recognized that they were in competition, pricing would have still risen. In the health arena prices are not driven by demand from willing buyers, but rather by suppliers in the face of unrestricted demand, unrelated to price. This is a clue pointing to one of our core findings, that health care, as it was then and as we know it today, is not a system driven by the forces of the free market. It is a game played by a different set of rules. We will revisit this issue of medical economics in a later chapter.

As more and more employers began offering health insurance as an employee benefit, whether paying the full premium or sharing the cost with their employees, pricing became a powerful tool for building market share. Experience rating was an effective strategy for "buying the business," where, in the employer-funded market, an employer group with low utilization could be offered an attractive premium rate. Many an employer entered into contracts as a result of this strategy only to have prices leap as utilization increased. This approach did not work in a community-pricing environment and it wasn't long before indemnity coverage was the predominant form of health insurance offered, with the Blues on board.

It should be noted that providing universal care was never an objective of the health insurance industry. From the beginning not all employers were willing and/or able to offer this type of coverage for their employees and many working men and women could purchase coverage only on an individual basis. Because the risk of an individual family could not be spread over a broad population, as could the coverage of a company workforce, the cost of individual coverage was typically greater than what one might get through group coverage. As a result there were large numbers of people from the ranks of the unemployed, the working poor and the elderly for whom health coverage was out of reach.

Employers who offered coverage as a benefit of employment were not immune from the rising cost of care and were faced with difficult decisions about continuation of the benefit. Taking away a benefit is something employers want to avoid, so faced with the rising cost of premiums, there were several options available to them, short of cancellation of the benefit. The first was to increase the percentage of the premium paid by the employee, the second was to modify the coverage, and a third was to tighten eligibility requirements. Typically these options meant higher deductibles and higher out-of-pocket limits for the employees and their families.

During this developmental period in the history of health insurance, the widespread availability of coverage contributed to the emergence of another significant change in health care. Gradually, as more people gained health insurance coverage, they remarkably began to dissociate themselves from the cost of care. People no longer had to worry about how they would be able to afford care in the event of major illnesses or injuries. Even though they would still be responsible for a portion of the cost of such care the cost no longer seemed to matter. As a result, the cost of the care required was no longer part of the decision criteria in the face of choices between one treatment alternative and another. This seemingly subtle change would have great impact on the ability of market forces to drive change in the health care arena.

The Last 50 years

Prior to the entrance of private medical insurers, practicing physicians made sparing use of assistants, whether a nurse or other support staff. In many cases the support staff consisted of the physician's wife and/or other members of his family. Many a physician's wife served as both nurse and office staff. As doctors with busy practices began to add support staff, the importance of cash payment was enhanced. It's one thing for a physician to accept payment in a form other than cash and quite another to offer to pay staff in similar currency. A nurse was, also, an economically driven enhancement. While the decision to employ a nurse was driven by the desire to improve the quality of care, it was also influenced by an enhanced ability to see more patients and, therefore, bill for more services. The nurse could take care of the little things and attend to details so that a greater portion of the physician's time could be devoted to patient care, which is, of course, the predominant revenue-generating activity.

As the practice of medicine became more sophisticated and as the telephone played an increasingly significant role, even more help was required. Help to keep records, and then help to find the records when needed. Help to answer the phone, to schedule appointments, take care of correspondence, pay bills and most importantly, bill for services rendered. The more complex the insurance filing process became and the more numerous the participation agreements, the more labor- and technology-intensive was the business. These changes happened gradually and each wave brought a more insistent need for cash. The physician's willingness to provide care to the indigent was no longer just the function of a charitable heart and an acknowledged responsibility to the community, rather it became a calculated business decision.

The irony is that it was easier to provide indigent care when there was no expectation of payment than it is now to deal with the Medicaid process or with other entitlement programs.

Through all of these changes the physician maintained a willingness to work with his patients, whenever their situations made payment difficult or impossible. The doctor felt a close personal relationship with his patients and had confidence, based upon demonstrated performance, that the patient would pay as much as they could as quickly as they were able. As insurance and other third party payers emerged it changed the whole nature of the business side of medicine.

Medicare and Medicaid

The decade of the sixties was a line of demarcation separating two distinct periods of American twentieth-century history and, as a result of events beginning in this period, the personality of the nation was forever altered. The 1960s were similarly significant for health care.

The growing problem of lack of coverage for the elderly eventually led to action. After years of debate and heated opposition from opponents of socialized medicine of any kind, Title 18 of the Social Security Act was passed, establishing Medicare. Almost unnoticed at the time, Title 19, which later became known as Medicaid, also passed. Both were to have enormous consequences for the nation. On the one hand, as a result of these programs the elderly and the poorest of the poor, often single mothers and their children, were given access to care. What could not have been anticipated was the far-reaching impact these programs would have on the business of medicine. One subtle but monumental result was the manner in which health insurance, Medicare, and Medicaid irrevocably changed the way providers bill for services. Any semblance of the informality characteristic of the expectations for payment on the part of providers prior to this time, evaporated and fee-for-service medicine was transformed into a zero-sum billing game with winners and losers.

It is difficult to overstate the degree to which this new way of looking at fee collection has adversely influenced the cost of health care. Now, nearly a half-century later, after several amendments and innumerable regulatory enhancements, the cost of these programs remains high and the system's complexity has reached new levels. As costs rose, the pressure on federal and state legislatures to reduce the tax burden grew and more often than not this led to constriction of service coverage and tightening of eligibility.[1] Most unsatisfactory is the reality that in spite of the billions of tax dollars spent on these programs the gap between those with access to care and those without seems wider still, as millions of people slip into the crevices.

Group Medical Practice

Other innovations of the time include the continued evolution of the group medical practice, whether single- or multi-specialty. While many physicians continued to practice as an independent entity, more and more doctors were gravitating to groups. Health care experienced the same pressure as that experienced in other segments of the business environment – that bigger is better. Across the whole nation the small independent retailers, grocers, pharmacies, gas stations, banks, manufacturers and distributors are being supplanted by larger competitors able to take advantage of greater buying power and other economies of scale. We live in the world of super stores and super-sizing. In health care this trend is affecting medical groups, hospitals, nursing homes and other providers.

In the groups, ranging from small to large, physicians joined together in some form of structured business arrangement, sometimes formal and at other times, not. The medical group might compensate physicians with salary or might utilize some type of revenue-sharing formula. Some groups are more accurately described as associations in which the physicians are paid directly from the revenue they generate after the costs of the association's pooled activities are allocated. Whether formal group or association, these structures allow physicians to share support staff, and to pool resources to provide other services to their combined patient population. The resulting economies of scale have paved the way for the appointment of professional managers to look after the business needs of the group and also have given groups a great deal of flexibility to seek innovative solutions in response to the needs of the community.

---

[1] A recent example can be found in the State of Indiana where, faced with budget deficits at the start of the year 2002, the State is contemplating reduction in Medicaid Benefits for prescription drugs.

The Business of Medicine

Within the practice of medicine it was the business side that was most directly affected by private health coverage, Medicare, and Medicaid. The success of a medical business entity was now judged on its ability to generate revenue. With ever-greater speed, escalations in the level of complexity demanded by insurers, payers and intermediaries were answered with a corresponding increase in the resources necessary to effectively bill for the provider's services. This, once again, meant more staff and more technology and, providers also began to place greater reliance on such external resources as consulting, accounting, legal and collection services followed more recently by software and hardware suppliers and service firms.

Every decision to purchase support from external resources results in a revenue drain which, when combined with discounted fee schedules, can change a practice P & L from black to red in a hurry. These forces serve to make group practice a much more attractive alternative. Not only do the economies of scale available to the group make it easier to invest in practice management support and technology, it also opens up the opportunity to make investments that generate revenue. Labs, x-ray, mammography and physical therapy are just a few examples. As one might expect the popularity of group practice has increased during this time period and it is a rare community that doesn't have both specialty and primary care groups, and in some cases, multi-specialty groups combining primary and specialty care.

As the HMO movement began to take root, medical groups emerged as an ideal source of providers.

Managed Care

The Kaiser-Permanente program, was an early provider of comprehensive care for a cross section of the population in exchange for a pre-paid fee, marking a break from the fee-for-service tradition. In a business context the Kaiser Group's strategy could be characterized as a form of vertical integration where the entity owns the entire chain of services from the first primary care contact to hospitalization and most everything in between. Kaiser was a model for the HMO (Health Maintenance Organization) movement that burst into the headlines in the 1970's, with presidential urging. As other "staff" model HMOs entered the market they, too, offered comprehensive coverage for their members for a prepaid fee and were staffed by physicians and other health care professionals who typically were employees of the enterprise.

The HMO concept placed providers at financial risk, thereby providing a monetary incentive for the HMO to maintain the health of their patients and control utilization of services. One of the objectives of this arrangement was to place the organization in a position, unique in the private-sector health industry, from which it could practice proactive rather than reactive medicine.

In the staff model HMO many of the employee physicians were paid a salary regardless of the number of patients seen or procedures performed. Without the pressure to generate revenues in the typical fashion (by loading up the schedule and cranking out billable services) the providers were theoretically free to concentrate on a wellness approach with emphasis on the prevention of illness and injury.

Other HMOs, rather than making the capital investment required in the staff model, chose to focus on selling prepaid coverage to employer groups and then to contract with professional and institutional providers for delivery of the care. Medical groups offered an ideal fit.

In the purest form of this "group model" the medical group was placed at financial risk typically through a capitation contract in which they were paid a flat monthly rate for each enrollee. This required a paradigm shift for physicians, as their financial success was now contingent upon their ability to change the way they approached the practice of medicine. No longer was it of value to generate billable activity, although this would prove a hard habit to break. The challenge now was to find the optimum use of the provider's time, balancing the need to treat illness and injury with the long-term benefit of early intervention, prevention and education. The idea was simple – provide a monetary incentive to physicians that rewards them for keeping the patient healthy, and it seemed to make perfect sense.

The medical group under a full-risk contract was responsible for purchasing any care that it was unable to provide from within. Most of the medical groups that participated as "at risk" providers also practiced fee-for-service medicine, a fact that added more complexity to the business side of their practice.

One of the key provisions of an HMO is that the enrollees are restricted to use of only HMO physicians for both primary and specialty care, and to hospitals and other ancillary providers owned, affiliated or under contract with the HMO. The primary care physician was asked to play the role of gatekeeper and was given the responsibility for managing the utilization of services for their patients. Under this gatekeeper arrangement the primary care doctor controls the utilization of not only his own resources but also those of other caregivers. The gatekeeper makes the decision to bring in a specialist and, also directs the case only to one of the approved specialty or ancillary providers. Without this type of control at the gate, the theory suggests, the HMO would be powerless to influence, let alone control utilization and it is this control that is key to the HMO's financial success.

Hospitals that entered the managed care arena, already reeling from the impact of "diagnostic related groups" (DRGs), suffered the impact of aggressive pressure to reduce the cost of care. Managed care's efforts focused on reducing the number of admissions and shortening length of stays with more frequent use of outpatient surgical centers and home health care. But it was not only in the area of admissions and length of stay that pressure was felt, but also in a number of other hospital services. More and more managed care organizations looked to free-standing urgent care clinics to reduce emergency room costs and many of the medical groups under contract to the HMO offered extended hours by creating night and evening clinics in their own facilities and sometimes opening their own free-standing urgent care facilities. Groups were also quick to open in-practice labs, x-ray and mammography units, all in an attempt to reduce the flow of revenue to outside providers.

Impact of the HMOs on Health Care

The managed care industry, HMOs in particular, receives too little credit for its significant role in reducing health care costs and also improving the way providers work together to provide quality care. Reductions in the length of hospital stays, increased utilization of out-patient surgical centers as well as utilization of other alternatives to hospitalization have had a positive impact on aggregate health care costs in this country. This contribution was made at great cost to the HMO movement which, has been bludgeoned for abuses while many of the positive contributions are ignored. HMOs provided a level of care that, for years, was branded as substandard; care that has since become the accepted standard. Physician pioneers in the emergence of HMOs were seldom popular among their fee-for-service counterparts.

Yet for all of its promise and substantial contributions to the health care industry the HMO concept remains controversial and has struggled to earn the confidence of the professional medical community and the general public. Attempts to ameliorate these concerns led to modified approaches such as the Independent Practice Association (IPA) which were built on a discounted fee-for-service model of the HMO concept. One of the most recognized problems and most unpopular features of HMOs was the limited selection of physicians. By allowing doctors to hold onto the fee-for-service approach these IPAs, in many cases physician-owned, were successful in recruiting large panels of doctors, often offering them an opportunity for equity in the company. This new approach did not obviate the need for utilization control, however, as the only way these plans could turn a profit was to reduce the cost of care. This could be accomplished in two ways, by discounting the fees for services and by controlling utilization. Comprehensive guidelines were provided to physicians to help them identify opportunities to keep costs down and the controls were placed at the end of the care delivery process, at which time the utilization data for each provider was reviewed.

While many of these HMOs were successful in growing enrollment, often significantly, meaningful controls were difficult to achieve and, to stay in business, these plans were generally forced to increase prices.

For the providers the IPA was viewed as a defensive strategy whereby the provider would accept a discounted payment for services in exchange for reducing the probability that patients would be lost to other managed care programs. In the mind of many physicians they were providing the same services to the same patients for less money.

The HMO industry was also hampered by other weaknesses in structure and design. It was not uncommon, for example, for salaried doctors to discover, as had salaried workers everywhere, that they were compensated whether productive or not. One would think it easy to deal with low productivity but so often physicians will back away from the responsibility of passing judgment on their peers, let alone apply sanctions. Physicians share an almost universal belief that the practice of medicine is as much an art as a science. As with any art form it is easy to critique but extraordinarily difficult to get inside the artist's head and understand fully what he had tried to convey.

Physicians share the artist's fears and few are immune from the worry that others will judge their work as somehow less than exemplary. Right or wrong, one of the best strategies to avoid such scrutiny on oneself is to cast few, if any, stones.

For generations physicians have been truly independent practitioners. Barring any extraordinary mistakes or consequences, physicians operated almost totally outside the scope of systematic review. Very few of their medical decisions were scrutinized let alone criticized. In the last several decades the predominant strategy to reduce health care costs, other than limiting the amounts of reimbursement, has been to control physician practice behavior. Insurance and managed care companies alike, do so by setting more and more complicated guidelines, by pre-certifying hospital admissions as well as coverage for some procedures, and by restricting "piggy-back" services that previously were approved without question.

Common sense would suggest that the most frequent physician complaint centers around reimbursement rates but complaints regarding the inhibitions doctors feel that keep them from practicing "the kind of medicine for which I was trained," may be even more numerous.

Lets review some of the reasons people give for the failure of the HMO movement.

As we have alluded, one of the ways in which the HMO movement failed to fulfill its promise as the saving force of health care, was its inability to win the hearts of fee-for-service physicians and woo them away from traditional modes of practice. Fee-for-service medicine is the practice modality of choice for providers because it is perceived to be the most profitable, because it offers the widest latitude and, demands minimal financial risk and accountability. A capable practitioner, who is also an average

33

businessperson, will simply pass their costs on to the payer, whether that be the cost of over-utilization or poor business decisions.

HMOs are not always price-competitive with traditional insurance or with PPO's and other hybrid offerings, when one compares only monthly premium rates. When comparing total cost to the enrollee's family, both premium and out-of-pocket costs, however, HMOs may compare favorably. The majority of covered persons come from employer sponsored plans. When faced with a decision in the open enrollment period few employees with an absence of serious health problems look beyond that portion of the premium rate that will be deducted from their paycheck.

One of the results of this enrollment bias was that the employees who found HMOs most attractive were often those whose families were dealing with some kind of serious, or at least aggravating health problem. The resulting adverse selection contributed significantly to the fiscal challenges facing health maintenance organizations. This phenomenon also impacted the characteristics of HMO enrollments. One of the consequences of small enrollments is that risks are not sufficiently spread to protect the HMO or its providers from the problems related to a disproportionate number of high cost cases.

We have already addressed the dissatisfaction of many with regard to the limited provider panels from which enrollees must select a family physician. Some will simply not change physicians and others who will accept the change, are unlikely to cease complaining about the decision they were compelled to make.

HMO contract negotiations are subject to the same market price pressures as their private insurance counterparts. Whether facilities, specialists, or other providers they look to the medical component of the CPI as the benchmark for increases in what they charge the HMO, giving only those organizations with huge market share a strategic advantage.

Other Managed Care Initiatives

In the decades since the emergence of HMOs as a viable player in the health care market place there have been other innovations that merit notice even if we can devote only passing mention. The two most prominent are Preferred Provider Organizations and employer self-funded health plans.

Preferred Provider Organizations have grown in popularity as they typically offer a wide network of providers who agree to offer pricing favorable to PPO enrollees. Preferred provider organizations are simply an agreement between the managed care company and providers where the PPO entity markets coverage to employee groups whose members receive higher coverage rates when they elect to utilize the plan's preferred providers. For many providers the PPO is also viewed as a defensive marketing strategy. The more listings for the provider the less likely he will lose patients whose employers have changed from one managed care company to another. In exchange for the listing the provider agrees to accept discounted reimbursement rates and to abide by the plans rules. PPOs place less emphasis on utilization review than the IPA/HMO.

Self-funded plans are initiated by employers seeking to eliminate the middleman to the extent possible. These employers will contract with a benefit administrator who will process claims and maintain utilization records. Typically such plans will then contract with a preferred provider network. These then, function much in the same way as any other preferred provider plan. Self-funded plans have become quite popular and there are few large employers that have not explored this avenue in meeting the coverage needs of their employees.

Although we refer to PPOs as managed care, providers within a PPO typically bill on a fee-for-service basis. The savings generated generally result more from the negotiated fee schedules rather than from utilization control, although pre-certifications and other utilization review are involved. The result is that fee-for-service is still the name of the game in health care for the vast majority of physicians.

The Hospital

The evolution of the modern hospital has been every bit as dynamic as other components of the health care system and one could argue that, particularly in the last several decades, hospitals have faced, perhaps the greatest challenges of all providers. Whether church related, private or municipal, hospitals were once the center of a community's health care activity. Moving beyond basic inpatient care, hospitals became the primary provider of a range of ancillary services to physicians. For many years hospitals were the only player with sufficient resources to offer operating rooms, emergency departments, labs, radiology, physical therapy and intensive care centers. Since the hospital offered the only game in town they could be assured their services would be widely used and that they would have a fair return on their investment. In those communities with more than one hospital, a facility's ability to offer the latest and best technology was paramount to its success in retaining the full complement of admitting physicians necessary to maximize occupancy. Maintaining the loyalty of the physician staff is essential to success.

Like other providers hospitals were in a billing game. The more expensive the technology the more expensive the care, and the more expensive the care the more aggressive the tactics of the payers, the bulk of whom were private and public insurers and managed care organizations, to control access and utilization.

As costs escalated, pressure to control cost led to a host of controls from DRGs (Diagnostic Related Groups), reductions in length of stay, and pre-certifications. Even more significant, concomitant with the evolution of managed care, was the emergence of alternative providers who promised to provide competing services at a more favorable price to the payer. Over the past three decades we have seen a proliferation of such providers from free-standing surgical centers, urgent care clinics, imaging centers and others.

On the hospital front local not-for-profit hospitals are being acquired at a rapid rate by large for-profit hospital systems, entities that often own and manage facilities across the country. This effectively moves strategic decision-making from the local administrative office to executive headquarters.

One of the most visible changes is the number of physicians who have sold their practices to one of the local hospitals or to the national hospital organization. For hospitals this strategy is a form of vertical integration and gives the hospital some control over the source of admissions. The perceived advantage of the hospital-based practice for the physician is freedom from the business distractions so they can focus on the practice of medicine. The hospitals also have many resources to offer the physicians and their patients while minimizing the number of significant technology investments necessary for a modern practice. And, last but certainly not least, the transaction offers an opportunity for cash and/or equity in the larger enterprise in exchange for the practice.

The competition between hospital- and physician-owned groups centers on the growing awareness of the power inherent in the physician's ability to control the flow of patients through the health care system and, of course, the knowledge that revenue follows the patient. Some physicians are beginning to view the hospital industry's foray into the practice of medicine as a threat.

The hospital business, like the medical practice, found itself immersed in a billing game played by varying sets of rules depending on whether the payer was private insurance, managed care, Medicare or Medicaid.

In the last several decades the migration of millions of middle class and affluent people out of the cities and into the suburbs has also played a role. Some of our oldest and finest hospitals found themselves stuck in declining neighborhoods surrounded by poverty and crime. Many of the strongest responded by building new facilities in the suburbs, offering attractive settings for a wide range of medical businesses including specialty and primary care group practices, along with labs and imaging centers and others.

During this same period, hard economic times and periods of double-digit inflation drove hospital costs upward in leaps while average lengths of stay were driven down by the pressures from the managed care industry.

Other Providers

The world of health care also changed for other providers, from ancillary providers such as labs, imaging centers, home health care centers, urgent care centers, out-patient surgical centers to long-term care facilities. The ancillary providers were seen as tremendous sources of revenues and became attractive acquisition targets for the private, for-profit hospital chains as well as for physician groups.

Long-term care facilities followed a path similar to that of hospitals as the small "mom and pop" facilities and many not-for-profit facilities were also acquired by business entities, often of regional or national scope.

Mel Hawkins

Quagmire

As we begin the twenty-first century the United States is burdened with a health care system so complex that it has become a source of frustration to virtually all of its players. While the words "managed care" provoke negative emotions of many of the systems players, the pressure to drive down cost keeps managed care in the forefront. The result is an atmosphere of tension throughout a system in which every new solution creates new problems. Rather than recognize that the problems with health care are systemic, the actors are prone to point the finger and assign the blame to others and no one seems ready to accept responsibility for their own contributions to the quagmire, let alone for finding solutions.

The truth is that all of the players have contributed to the problems of the system. The health care dilemma is not the fault of the HMO movement nor is it the result of an insatiable greed for profits on the part of physicians. If only it were that simple. As cliché as it may be the software analogy describes health care best. It is a system that has been twisted, and squeezed, modified and adapted so many times to address so many divergent issues that it has become a non-system. It is enormous, complex, rigid and unresponsive and over the years we have forgotten the systems' most basic purposes. We have lost sight of whom health care exists to serve.

This description of health care as a system out of control provides a perfect point of embarkation for our systems-thinking approach.

A ninety-five year old woman living in Illinois is only now beginning to experience the health problems typically resulting from the aging process. This individual had lived in her own apartment, albeit a subsidized senior housing complex, for seventeen years. She lived as a fully independent adult caring for her own needs. Prior to her retirement twenty years earlier she had devoted thirty years to a career in the billing office of one of the local hospitals during the pre-computer age. Since her retirement, Social Security has been her sole source of income, augmented by a modest savings in local financial institutions. As is typical of the diminishing population of Americans of her time, she is from a generation that diligently pays her bills with cash and borrows money from no one.

While her health problems are more irritating than dangerous, they require treatment and she is stunned by the costs of care and by the speed with which the dollars accumulate. Neither the prices nor the processes bear even a slight resemblance to the business of health care with which she was familiar. The emotional stress of discovering how incompetent she is in a venue in which she had experienced considerable success and for which she was esteemed, was devastating. The more the young billing clerks try to explain and the more her insurance agent, friends and family attempt to both educate and assure her, the more confused and depressed she becomes.

Most disturbing of all in this story is that this proud elder stateswoman, so positive in her thoughts and so full of energy has suffered an emotional trauma every bit as damaging as a serious medical problem. As her hope and energy diminish so too does her physical strength and medical problems begin to appear in inverse proportion to her emotional decline.

In September of 2001 an 81-page booklet was published entitled, "Medicare & You 2002." The booklet's purpose is to provide basic information about Medicare benefits, choosing a health care plan, and announcing new ways to get information. Mercifully her family chose to spare her the frustration of trying to make sense of it all.

CHAPTER 3

WHY DOES THE SYSTEM FAIL?

Let's begin with a fresh examination of American health care with the same scientific detachment that is applied toward the study of disease and the development of new treatments and new medicines. Let's also reconfirm that our objective is to gain a thorough understanding of the system; a grasp that will shift focus from symptoms exhibited by the system to one intended to shed the light of day on root causes. Understanding the root causes is vital if we intend to do more than patch the existing system. We must lay the foundation for a new system, constructed to our own specifications and engineered, like any automated system, to give us the outcomes we seek.

The problems of health care, we suggest, begin with our most basic assumptions about the health care system. The conventional wisdom purports that health care is a private good delivered in a free-market system and is influenced by the same forces of supply and demand that drive the American consumer-market economy. Critics of health care, particularly those critical of managed care, attribute spiraling costs to the insatiable hunger for profits on the part of providers, both professional and institutional, as well as on the part of insurance and managed-care companies.

Pat and Hugh Armstrong and their colleague Dr. Claudia Fegan write:

> *"American health care is at a crossroads. In the past fifty years, the profession of medicine has become the business of medicine and many people are unhappy with the result. The mission to relieve pain and suffering has been supplanted by the drive to maximize profits and the cost has been tremendous. Along the way, innocence and idealism have been lost, trust has eroded, and health care professionals find themselves uncertain as to who they are to serve" (Armstrong 1998).*

That innocence and idealism have been lost is difficult to dispute, as is the assertion that trust has eroded. The fact that so many Americans go without medical care certainly confirms that we have forgotten whom we exist to serve. What is not so clear is the genesis of this condition and one of the basic messages of this book is that the quest for profits has precious little to do with the breakdown of some of the basic tenets of health care. Neither is health care's crisis a consequence of some inherent flaw in the free-market system.

We offer an alternative hypothesis, one that suggests that at least a portion of health care's dysfunctionality results from misplaced expectations. Typically the efficacy of health care, a system that has evolved within the context of health care viewed as a private good traded in a free-market economy, is judged against our expectations of health care viewed as a public good to be distributed to all citizens. It seems odd that we would judge a system for its inadequacy in this area when the rules we as a society have established limit access to care to those who can afford it and limit coverage for those who cannot to the few Americans who meet the narrow criteria for eligibility for public assistance. Health care cannot meet expectations that are so at odds with the manner in which the game is played.

Think of the consequences of misplaced expectations from another perspective. We may well get frustrated that the applications software we purchased to perform one set of functions fails us when we attempt to apply it to other activities. It is possible, for example, to produce letters and other documents using one of the popular spreadsheet packages that were purchased to help us perform various analyses. We've learned, however, that word processing software will perform these functions far more effectively and efficiently. We don't moan about the poor performance of the spreadsheet software, we simply acquire a word processing package and use the spreadsheet software for the purpose for which it was designed.

Healthcare's failure can be primarily attributed to two causes. The first is our unwillingness or inability, it doesn't matter which, to resolve the public- versus private- good dichotomy. The second is our lack of understanding of the role of economics in health care. As will be explained in some detail in a later section, it is our assertion first, that health care is a public good and second, although it appears on the surface to be contradictory, that health care is shielded from the influence of market forces and cannot, therefore, benefit from them.

Many of us have, at one time or another, gone to great lengths to customize software so that it can be used in new ways to perform new tasks. It doesn't take long for us to learn that although this solution may work in the short run, eventually the tool's performance begins to deteriorate. The more programming modifications we make to correct this poor performance, the more complicated the system becomes until finally, it has become rigid and dysfunctional. The American health care system has been similarly degraded. In the case of health care, the damage is magnified by the fact that fifty years of tinkering, of modifications, and of reforms have been driven by a fundamental misdiagnosis. What we have inherited is a system that costs too much, serves too few people, and is too complicated for many players in the health care game.

In this section we will address some of the specific shortcomings of the U.S. Health Care system. We must acknowledge that there are many positive things to be said about health care in America, and in our zest to purge the system of its failings, we must not lose sight of the system's strengths. Nevertheless, the criticisms are many and well documented. One survey found that dissatisfaction levels about such issues as the quality of care, the delivery process, the cost of care, and the belief that providers and insurers are more concerned about profits than the quality of care, ranged from 64 to 87 percent (National Coalition on Health Care, 1997). Most of the issues we will be discussing overlap one another and are often difficult to isolate. We will review them in broad strokes in the balance of this chapter. In later chapters many of these issues will be discussed in greater detail.

Fee-For-Service Versus Managed Care

For those who can afford to pay for their care and for those who are covered by health insurance the quality of health care has been viewed as excellent. In the past two decades, with the increasing presence of managed care, irrespective of form, the quality of health care provided to the patients of managed-care organizations (MCOs) has been called into question. There are complaints from patients that providers cut corners to reduce or control costs; that access to providers is limited to only those approved by the managed care organization; and that access to specialists is restricted by gatekeepers. There are complaints from physicians of loss of control;

too much authority in the hands of non-providers who are far removed from the point of delivery; and, of course, there are concerns about lost income. Often the same physicians and the same hospitals that care for patients under the traditional fee-for-service model provide much of the care given through managed care organizations? What is different? The rules of the game and the manner of compensation are different and these are the things that drive provider choices and behavior. We need to understand the relationship between practice patterns and method of payment.

Critics of managed care point out that the incentives for managed care reward physicians for providing less care, thus creating a conflict of interest for physicians. Advocates would argue that physicians in managed care are rewarded for preserving the health of their patients. Critics of the traditional fee-for-service world of medicine suggest that the opposite is true. The incentives in a FFS practice reward providers for delivering more care, which also creates a conflict of interest. (Wong, 1998).

In the managed care environment providers are prepaid. Providers in managed care organizations earn profits only by controlling utilization and the outward flow of revenue. Every dollar spent on services of specialists, hospitals and other non-primary care providers is a dollar of revenue lost to the gatekeeper and to the MCO.

In the fee-for-service arena the only way providers get paid is to perform a billable service and then successfully collect payment, an objective that is far from automatic. FFS physicians are competing with private insurers in a zero-sum game in which the denial of a claim is a win for the insurer and a financial loss for the provider. The converse is also true that a paid claim represents a win for the provider at the expense (loss) of the insurer. The FFS venue is one in which win/win opportunities, if they exist at all, are rare.

What adds to the complexity of health care is that many providers practice in both venues, and have both FFS and MC patients and they must take time to be certain which set of rules apply.

We would suggest that the interests of providers and patients are parallel in neither delivery system. The challenge, then, is to create an environment in which the interests of patients and providers are parallel. We will return to this issue of merging the interests of both patients and providers at a later point, as this objective is core to the logic of the system we will propose.

Rising Cost

Over the last half-century the rise in health care costs can, in large part, be attributed to a cost-based reimbursement process that was virtually unrestrained. As a provider's costs rose it was, relative to the present, a simple matter to pass them on to the third-party payer. Increased fees, charges and reimbursements in provider contracts were routinely tied to the medical component of the consumer price index and, for most of the last half century, the rate of the medical inflation has been consistently higher than that of the overall CPI. This created a self-perpetuating cycle in which the medical costs rose faster than inflation, a cycle that continues to this day. In September of 2001, for example *the Los Angeles Times* reported the findings of a Kaiser Family Foundation Report that indicate that, from the Spring of 2000 to the Spring of 2001, *"employers' health costs increased 11 percent…"* In recent years the driver of health costs has become less obvious and more complex although these same forces are still in the background. There are no simple answers in health care.

We have selected two components for this discussion. The first is the income expectation of physicians and other providers, and the second is the "billing game" that dominates the business side of medicine, including significant portions of the managed care industry. Both of these issues must be viewed from health care's genesis in the private sector where the services provided were viewed as a private good.

It is common knowledge that physicians rank among the most highly paid professionals in the United States. While this may be a source of irritation to some people, the reality is that physicians' income expectations are high and this is unlikely to change. It is a simple logic. There is a great deal of money in health care and physicians play the central role in the administration of care to patients. It is difficult to imagine how we could even have a health care system without physicians. How well physicians are compensated is a function of both the primacy of their role and, also, the value we place on the contribution they make.

Consider how hard it is to become wealthy while educating children or keeping the peace. However much we admire the contributions of teachers, police officers and firefighters, what we pay these men and women speaks eloquently to the issue of their relative value compared to some other professions. Whether or not our priorities should be re-ordered is a matter for discussion at another time. With regard to health care, is this fair or are physicians over-compensated?

Physician compensation did not just happen, it evolved as the role physicians play evolved and it has been influenced by supply and demand. As important as the contributions of teachers and public safety officers may be, for example, there is a significant portion of the adult population of men and women who have the physical and intellectual capability to perform these roles. While the commitments and sacrifices necessary to obtain the education and training for these roles is not insignificant, there seem to be more than enough candidates to meet the needs of the community.

The percentage of the population having the capacity to master the physical and intellectual demands of a medical education, on the other hand, is quite small, as is the relative number of individuals willing to endure the sacrifices and demands of either the training or the practice of medicine. As motivated and committed as the vast majority of our physicians may be, there are few for whom the income potential of medicine was not a factor in their career choices.

Medicine is a poignant example of a situation where we get what we pay for. Medicine gets the cream of the crop because the incentives are powerful and, as a result, young people must compete rigorously for the opportunity. If we were to significantly reduce the potential compensation for physicians, it seems reasonable to predict that both the number and quality of the candidates for medical school would decline considerably.

The problem is not that we pay physicians too much, but rather that we abuse those in the fields of education and public safety by not adequately valuing their efforts and contributions. When one compares the level of excellence in health care with that of law enforcement and education, isn't it sad that we don't apply the same logic. Not wishing to denigrate the efforts of thousands of public safety officers and teachers, just imagine how the caliber of the men and women entering these professions would soar if we were to raise the starting salaries to $50,000 or even $75,000 per year. Make no mistake, any solution to the American health care system that significantly reduces earnings of providers will have an adverse effect on the quality of health care.

To a degree far beyond that which is the case in education and public safety, money is the driving force of the present health care system. On the one side is the power of the providers seeking to make money in health care and on the other are those who would try to control how much revenue those providers retain, not for the benefit of society but for their own profit. It is here that even the most intelligent and well-educated Americans arrive at the erroneous conclusion that it is the quest for profits that is at the core of health care's ills. We suggest an alternate conclusion. The problem is not that physicians make a lot of money, the problem is the way the incentives are structured. The problem is not that insurance and managed care companies strive for profitability, the problem is that they exist at all.

It has been suggested that the workday of a quarter of US health care workers is consumed by paperwork, and that this number continues to grow (Armstrong, 1998). These actors provide no care nor do they provide direct support for caregivers. Instead they consume enormous resources billing for services, restricting access, limiting coverage, setting utilization standards, building bureaucracies and engaging providers in a competition for revenue; the competition we have referred to as the billing game. The prevalent insistence that the core problem of health care is profits continues to draw our focus away from the systemic forces that are the true drivers of health care. These forces are economic, but of a convoluted sort. One might compare economics in health care to a drug that when properly administered will produce miraculous results, but which functions as a poison when misapplied. The problem is not the medication, but the application. We will devote significant space in a later chapter to the entire issue of medical economics.

For our purposes here, we have said that fee-for-service medicine is a billing game – a zero-sum game to be precise. A zero-sum game is one in which every win must be offset by a comparable loss so that the value of the win minus the value of the loss equals zero. Health care functions under a cost-based reimbursement system or more accurately, a cost-plus reimbursement system in which providers strive to generate sufficient revenue to cover their costs plus a desired profit margin. Health care differs from the typical consumer market in that only a portion of a provider's fee is paid directly to the provider by the user/patient. The larger portion of the provider's revenue is funneled through an insurer, whether private or public, that is a third party to the exchange of health services for a fee and, that must siphon off sufficient revenue to cover its own costs plus a desired profit margin. Every dollar that is not paid to the provider remains with the insurer, creating a competition for each dollar.

In health care, resources are scarce and there is insufficient revenue to fully fund all players' operations. When either party's share falls short of meeting its requirements there is a measurable increase in the pressure for the provider to bill for more activity and to raise fees; and, for the insurer, in some combination, to raise premiums, reduce benefits, tighten eligibility and increase market share.[2]

Increasing market share involves price competition, often in the form of "buying the business." Commonly, new accounts garnered via this process will see significant premium increases from their insurer or MCO in subsequent contract years. Securing a book of business in this manner places much pressure on the insurer to reduce their claims paid. Feeling the pressure on the provider side, providers work harder to bill more services to maintain their revenue stream and so the cycle continues.

The entire process is grossly inefficient and adds to the aggregate cost of health care at the same time it reduces the value the patient receives for each dollar paid for health care. The American patient is the big loser in the "billing game" and no one truly wins.

Market Forces

The conventional wisdom attributes at least a portion of the blame for healthcare's rising cost to the profit motive and to the characteristics of a free-market economy. We would submit that the opposite is true. One of the root causes of the health care's rising cost structure is that free-market forces, including the profit motive, are

---

[2] The author's family has experienced a recent example of this practice as, effective January 1, 2002, the deductible on the family's health insurance coverage has been increased from $200 per person to $500.

not utilized consistently, but even this is a gross understatement. The best description we can offer of health care viewed as an economic model is that it is convoluted and schizophrenic.

Think for a minute about health care within the context of a consumer economy. We will use the world of retail as a basis of comparison. We all understand how the system works and we know the rules of the game. When we have a need for something, or simply want something we go to a store, open a catalog, or pull up an e-tailer site on the Internet and purchase whatever it is we desire. Our decisions are influenced by what we want (demand), what is available (supply), the price (which is driven by the relationship of supply and demand) and, by our ability to pay. Within this framework we make decisions concerning what we will purchase and no one understands better than we whether our wants and needs are worth the price we must pay. A free market economy is also self-regulating in the sense that producers of goods and services who fail to keep their customer's satisfied are naturally culled from the marketplace. Sellers must perform in order to survive.

Think, on the other hand, how such decisions in health care are made and note the comparisons.

As in the consumer market, in health care the individual still determines that a need exists; we have an ache, pain, or some other symptom. If it bothers us sufficiently we conclude that a medical problem exists and we seek out care. Once we arrive at the provider's place of business, however, we relinquish responsibility for decision-making almost entirely. The physician examines us, listens to us as we describe our complaint and its symptoms and then he tells us what we need. He may recommend diagnostic tests, surgical or other treatment procedures, medications or some combination thereof. We may accept or reject the physician's decision, but for all practical purposes we depend on the professional caregiver to assess our needs and tell us how they can best be met. We delegate this responsibility not because we are apathetic, but because we lack the training and knowledge to make that determination ourselves. We will, however reserve the right to reject the provider's recommendations, but as our respect for the knowledge of our physician is high, rarely does this occur.

Once we accept the decision of the physician with respect to the treatment plan, we are faced with financial consequences. If we can afford the cost of the care or have health insurance coverage of some kind the physician arranges the delivery of care. In the majority of instances the individual is covered by a health insurance policy of some kind. Even though we understand that we will be responsible for a portion of the bill, we know there is a limit on the amount of our out-of-pocket expense and that our insurance will pick up the balance, no matter how much it may be. Because of this insurance protection, combined with our faith in the physician and the sense of urgency we feel when our health is at risk, we rarely if ever let the cost of the procedure influence our decision to accept or reject the physician's treatment plan.

Now envision this same process in a retail venue. We think we need something new. It may be clothing, a piece of furniture, a television or a new automobile, we're not really sure. We go to our local retail professional and describe our longing. Our retailer listens to us and then begins to formulate a purchase plan that will, in his judgment, satisfy our want or need. He decides for example that we need a new CD system with the latest in sophisticated technology. We have a right to question his decision or to refuse his purchase recommendation, but we have faith in him so we are prepared to follow his direction. He is the expert and has always been right before.

Not only does our retailer diagnose our need, he also offers to sell his products as a solution to our needs. Next, he outlines the price that he will charge for the CD system. Fortunately, we have retail insurance that, after a small deductible a portion of which has already been met, will cover the majority of the cost of our new sound system and, as a result, the cost of the product has little if any influence on our decision to purchase.

How would capitalism work if this were the process for making all consumer decisions? The customer has little responsibility in the process. The seller of the goods and services tells us what we will purchase and what it will cost and we have insufficient information to question his recommendation. The payer, a third party to the transaction, also has little ability to influence the retailer's decisions and recommendations and is virtually obligated to pay for our sound system. The payer may have established a list of prices that they have agreed to pay or, items they will not cover, but beyond this they have minimal recourse. Even this approved price schedule has nominal influence on the retailer as he already knew what the scheduled price would be and, furthermore, was in a position to add a few accessories to the transaction, items that the insurance will also cover.

A free-market system is made up of buyers, who are both willing and knowledgeable, and sellers who must satisfy those wants and needs. The prices of consumer goods and services are driven by the demand of the buyer and the supply or availability of the specific goods and services that the buyer/customer demands. The forces of supply and demand gravitate toward an equilibrium that creates a stable marketplace. A free market is also a self-regulating system that weeds out sellers who are unable to offer the goods and services that are in demand at a price the customer is willing to pay. As demand is a dynamic force the successful seller must also be able to, first, continuously improve the quality of the goods and services he produces and secondly, be able to offer new goods and services in response to incessant shifts in demand. As noted above, a free-market economy is also unforgiving of sellers who cannot anticipate and adapt to changes in demand.

Another powerful force in a free-market economy is the profit motive of the seller. It is this desire for profits, and the need for profits, that motivates sellers to invest their scarce resources of land, labor and capital, in an effort to meet customer demands. Imagine an economy in which sellers were apathetic toward consumer demands and chose to sell only those goods and services it was convenient for them to produce.

It should be clear that health care, a system in which the seller of services creates his own demand and, virtually, sets his own prices, is anything but a free-market system and is, in fact, immune to the forces of capitalism. Health care is a system, but one driven by an entirely unique set of forces, about which we have little understanding.

That our health care system is failing to meet our expectations is a result, not of the greed of providers, but rather of these unique forces. Our metaphor about medicine prior to the discovery of bacteria's role in living organisms describes the American health care system quite accurately. Until we understand the forces that drive and influence health care and use that knowledge to address its problems we will be no more successful at curing its ills than were physicians of the dark ages in treating the ills of their patients.

Access

The growing group of people without coverage includes a surprising cross section of the population. At the lowest end of the economic continuum are those Americans living in hard core poverty, a group that includes: homeless men, women and children and, also the hard core unemployed. Although a portion of these people may qualify for coverage under Medicaid, large numbers of them receive little if any care.

As the circle widens, the numbers grow significantly. Included are the unemployed, some of whom had coverage from their former employers and some of whom have never enjoyed health coverage.

Another group, far more broad, is those whom we often label as "working poor." This segment includes Americans who earn a low wage and work for employers that are unable or unwilling to offer a healthcare benefit.

In total, roughly fifteen percent of the population falls somewhere on this list of Americans who are disenfranchised with respect to health care. This is a staggering proportion of the American population. For these people it doesn't matter whether we have the best providers and the best facilities, nor does it matter how many billions of dollars are spent on health care in our country.

Another key issue in our discussion of access to care is the disproportionate number of minorities in the rolls of the uninsured and under-served. Writing in the Journal of the American Medical Association, Trevino, Moyer, Valdez and Stroup-Bentham report that *"there is a longstanding pattern of racial and ethnic disparity in the access to and the delivery of health care services in the United States"* (Trevino, Moyer et al 1997).

How can these men and women fully embrace the American dream when they are barred from health care's door? Although there are many things that contribute to the widening alienation and disenfranchisement of America's poor and minority populations, the lack of access to quality health care must be near the top of the list. Can we reasonably expect children to learn when serious, unattended health problems dominate the environment in which they live? Can we reasonably expect working men and women to be fully productive and to learn new skills and new technology when they suffer from illness or injury improperly treated or, when they worry about getting the care that their sick child requires? That this group grows with each passing day should prompt a clarion call.

Healthcare Expenditures and Other Cost Drivers

It is estimated that 13 percent of our country's gross domestic product (GDP) is currently spent on health care. In 1999 health care costs were estimated to be just under $1.2 trillion or roughly $4,250 for every man, woman or child in the United States. How is it that we can spend this extraordinary sum and not address the needs of the whole population?

As we have discussed, the answers are many and they are complicated. We assert that the traditional fee-for-service approach, where providers are paid for billable services extended to the patients, is a primary driver of health care's price tag. We also submit that the managed care industry has not been successful in reversing the direction of rising cost. What limited success managed care has enjoyed in managing costs more effectively has come with a price tag. Another significant factor, as has been mentioned, is that a significant portion of health care expenditures pay for activity that is not directly related to the care of patients.

As noted in an earlier paragraph some suggest that twenty-five percent of the time spent by health care workers in the U.S. is devoted to paperwork (Armstrong, 1998). In a study commissioned by the American Hospital Association, Pricewaterhouse-Coopers found that *"… for various stages of [hospital] care of a typical patient, paperwork adds at least 30 minutes to every hour of patient care provided and, in some settings, adds an hour of paperwork to every hour of patient care"* (Pricewaterhouse Coopers, 2001). This suggests that a full third of hospital expenditures are routinely allocated to what we have labeled as non-value-added activity.

Think of the billions of dollars that go to pay the salaries of all the people who work for the insurance companies, the managed care companies, the third-party administrators, the collection agencies, and government agencies with health care responsibilities. Think of the billions more that go to pay for the non-payroll costs of these organizations.

Add also the dollars spent by professional, institutional, and ancillary providers to cover the cost of filing claims just so these providers can be paid for the services they deliver. How much care could be purchased if all of these dollars could be diverted to pay for direct care of patients? There can be no doubt that a significant contributor to the cost of health care in the United States is the health care system itself, with all of its complexity.

Other forces also influence health care costs. The incredible advancements in technology play a significant role, as the substantial cost of this technology must be covered by the prices of health care services. Beyond the desire to provide new and innovative diagnostics and treatments, the rationale for investments in medical technology is almost always the increased billing opportunities these technologies represent. These technologies have had an enormous impact on the quality of care. In business and industry the cost of new technology may be all or partially offset by gains in productivity. This has not been the case in health care. We will address this issue more fully in a chapter devoted to medical economics.

The rising proportion of specialists in the physician population also contributes as the services offered by these providers are typically more costly than primary care (Shi and Shin, 2001). In a sense, specialists also create their own demand, as it is difficult for a primary care physician to justify performing a procedure when a specialist with advanced training is available.

Ever-increasing expenditures for medical malpractice insurance is also a driver of cost increases as are the expenditures providers must pay for legal representation for medical malpractice claims.

With every new reform comes a new layer of complexity and, as a result, the percentage of the finite health care dollars allocated to the direct care of patients is reduced.

Impersonalization of Care.

More and more patients feel distanced from their physicians and yearn for the days when they had a personal relationship with their doctor. The way our health care system functions, however, makes this incredibly difficult to attain. The obstacles to such relationships can be found on both ends of the stethoscope.

In addition to the mobile society that the United States has become, where individuals and families relocate a number of times in each generation, people no longer have full control of the physician selection process. For those Americans covered under an employer-sponsored health coverage plan the choice of physician may be dictated by the coverage the employer elects to purchase. If the employer chooses an HMO for example, the employee must choose from a relatively narrow list of providers who are employees or sub-contractors for the HMO. Those employees whose current physician is not on the provider list are forced to change physicians or face loss of coverage, an option that few can afford. Employees required to choose from the provider list of a PPO might have better odds that their family doctor is a participant but this is far from a certainty.

The situation is then complicated by the fact that each year the employer has an opportunity to choose a different type and source of coverage, when it is time to renew the contract with the insurer or managed care company. Whenever a new carrier is selected there is a possibility that employees will be forced, once again, to change physicians.

As difficult as it is for patients to get to know a new physician every few years, it is even more challenging for the physician who may have two thousand patients on whom to keep tabs. Couple this with increasing pressure placed on service fees by the insurer/payers and the challenge is made more difficult. In order to grow their revenue and maintain their profit levels these providers must enter the health care game where success is measured in billable services. Economic success means maximizing the number of patients seen and services offered and that means less time spent talking and listening to patients. As much as physicians may regret their time-allocation decisions, these choices become easier when they see a steady stream of patients joining and then leaving their practice. Why risk reduced billings when relationships of any significant depth are impossible for all but a few patients? Like it or not, loyalty breeds loyalty.

Within the practices of specialty physicians this impersonalization is even more acute as often, a specialist may see the patient in a conscious state only once or twice during the brief life of the relationship.

Government Performance

There are some things that government does well but most Americans agree that there are many things government attempts to do with unsatisfying results. Health care is one of those activities. While government's motives might have been noble, the delivery of health care requires more than government's have to offer. As with the insurance and managed care industry, government's involvement almost always results in increased costs and increased bureaucracy. There are many talented people in government but the problem is structural. Even if government was blessed with the professional and business skills required, it is not structured in a manner that enables leadership to make the medical and business decisions that are required. Neither is government capable of making these decisions in a timely manner.

A successful American health care system will be one that minimizes the role of government.

So What Do We Do?

How is it that so few results have been generated by so much effort on the part of so many of our nation's most intelligent and imaginative leaders? With all of these issues a solution that will provide comprehensive, high quality medical care to the masses is possible only if we are willing to approach the challenge from a new direction and with a vision that results from a paradigm shift. That paradigm shift or new mental model must begin with resolution of the most basic question: Is health care a public or private good?

SECTION II
THE SOLUTION

What should the new system promise? How will providers be compensated for care given? Is it possible to create a system that can operate as a free market, thus minimizing the role of government? How will we provide care under a new system and how will the system work? What will the new system mean to patients and providers, and will it change the way they live and work? How do we overcome the extraordinary obstacles that will make implementation so difficult?

In broad strokes we want a system that:

- Provides comprehensive health care and prescription drugs to all American citizens
- Offers patients a free choice of primary care physician while leaving the existing provider system intact
- Permits physicians to practice quality medicine, free from interference of public and private bureaucrats
- Reduces the rate of increase of health care costs if not the aggregate annual expenditures.

- Utilizes free market forces to assure quality, internal to the process, obviating the need for external controls that were formerly imposed by the insurance industry, managed care, and the Health Care Finance Administration; and
- Limits the role of government to the few things governments do well.

The American health care system is "failing," charges a devastating report by an expert panel at the Institute of Medicine (IOM).

"Health care today harms too frequently and routinely fails to deliver its potential benefits," concludes the IOM in "Crossing the Quality Chasm: A New Health System for the 21st Century," issued in March. The institute is part of the National Academies established by Congress.

"Americans should be able to count on receiving care that uses the best scientific knowledge to meet their needs," says William C. Richardson, chair of the committee writing the report and president of the W.K. Kellogg Foundation in Battle Creek, Mich. "For too many patients, the health care system is a maze, and many do not receive the services from which they would likely benefit."

The report says the health system suffers from a lack of coordinated, comprehensive services, resulting in both the wasteful duplication of efforts and unaccountable gaps in care.

The report recommends revamping the entire health system over the next decade to encourage teamwork among professionals and to make patient needs and preferences the centerpiece of care (Institute of Medicine 2000).

CHAPTER 4

A PUBLIC OR A PRIVATE GOOD?

The entire health care dilemma in the United States comes down to a simple question. Is health care a public good, in which case it is something to which all Americans are entitled? Or, is health care a private good? Private goods are products and services, produced for a profit and that consumers purchase as a matter of choice, when and if they can afford it.

How can the health care dilemma in our country be reduced to such a simple broth? Stop and think for a moment. Why are we even concerned about health care? In earlier sections we acknowledged that we believe the U.S. has the best physicians, hospitals, nurses and ancillary providers. We also recognized that the pharmaceutical industry has produced a stream of remarkable new medicines to treat and alleviate the ailments of Americans. These are not the source of our dissatisfaction. Nothing is perfect but overall we are pleased with these components of the system.

So again we ask: "why are we disenchanted with the health care delivery system in the United States?" Some will be quick to say it is because the cost of health care is out of control and/or, because the system fails to meet the needs of more that forty million Americans. It is the thesis of this work that, as important as these issues may be, they are only symptoms and not the underlying cause. So what is the real issue?

Why is access to health care of any more concern than access to any other consumer product or service? Why don't we, for example, feel distress that 270 million Americans are unable to purchase a Cadillac, Lexus or some other luxury car? Should this not cause our blood to boil? Of course not, because we recognize that automobiles and other consumer goods and services are private goods available only to those who can afford to pay the price.

Someone said that *"in Europe health care is a right of citizenship and owning firearms is a privilege. In the United States owning firearms is a right of citizenship and access to health care is a privilege. "* Is this what the American people want?"

We have accepted the designation of public good for education, for police and fire protection and for national defense and there is no question about these services. When we call the local fire department the last thing we would expect is for them to pull up and ask to see our "fire insurance" card before they will turn on their hoses. If a child comes from a poor family we don't bar the door to the public school. We accept that the child is not only entitled to an education but we also recognize that it is in the best interests of our community that the child be educated. We may not always be satisfied with the quality of that education, but it is universally available, nevertheless.

Let's return to our question. Is health care a public or a private good? If health care was a private good we would not look askance when a sick child goes without medical attention because his or her family has no money with which to pay. If health care was truly a private good we wouldn't lose a moment's sleep with the knowledge that our neighbor cannot afford the care needed to treat his injuries from an automobile accident.

We may not have labeled health care, like education and public safety, as a public good but our actions speak eloquently.

What difference does it make, one might ask, whether we call health care a public good, a private good, or any kind of good at all? As we are about to see it makes all the difference in the world. It changes everything.

As we discussed in the last chapter, one of the core reasons the health care system is so complex and expensive is because all of the rules of the system are established on the premise that health care is a private good for which people must pay. Our dissatisfaction with the system is nothing more than a function of our misplaced expectations. There is an adage that says that we cannot have an argument unless we agree on a common premise. This same axiom of logic applies to health care. We will never be successful in our noblest reform efforts as long as those efforts are guided by logic constructed on a false premise. It is this author's belief that health care is and must be a public good.

The solution, once we accept health care as a service to be provided to all Americans regardless of their ability to pay, is to re-design our health care system to provide care to all Americans. It should be obvious that in doing so we will end up with a system remarkably different than that which we have today. We certainly will want to retain those aspects of the system that add value, but there are many other characteristics of our current health care delivery system that add no value and provide no utility. These must be discarded, but we will want to take great care that we don't discard things of value and it is not necessarily easy to distinguish between things that are needed and those that are not.

Anyone who has tried to clean out his attic, garage or basement can understand the challenge. If we haven't made an effort to think about what we need it is difficult to discard any of the possessions we have accumulated. We must make this same effort before we approach the task of re-constructing our health care system.

We can feel reasonably certain that few if any Americans want to lose any of those things that we have identified as being the best. On the other hand we could do without the complexity of the system and without activities that add cost but produce precious little value.

In thinking about health care in the context of market justice versus social justice, the latter is characterized as viewing health care as a basic right. Further that the distribution of care should be governed by need, and not by ability to pay. This view of health care as a social resource also assumes that the delivery of medical care requires the active involvement of government; that government is, in fact, better able to distribute care equitably. (Shi and Singh 2001)

This author would suggest to you that this is an erroneous assumption. There is no reason why universal health care cannot be delivered by private entities. What we need government to do is to collect and distribute tax dollars to pay for universal care. We can then use a little imagination to find a way to provide the care using private sources, without the bureaucracy that can so effectively constrain public endeavors. We can, in fact, structure the system so that it operates like a free market and benefits from free market forces.

In the chapters that follow we will reveal what we believe to be a unique solution, one that applies all the lessons of the past century. We will re-examine health care, viewed as an economic system, from the premise that health care is, indeed, a public good. We will show how this system will work, how much it will cost and how we will pay for it. We will discuss the roles of the players including the role of the physician, both primary care practitioner and specialist. How

Mel Hawkins

this new system will impact on all of the players, both individual and institutional, will be also discussed.

In the final section of the book we will take the next logical step and explore the challenges certain to face a proposal of such unprecedented change. And, last of all, we will lay out a strategy for gathering the support necessary to bring the vision of universal health care to the American people.

A family medical practice invests considerable money to train its insurance clerks on the latest collections and claims processing technology, as well as on the latest collection strategies. Nevertheless, the mistakes of careless, inexperienced or poorly trained staff who fail to play the insurance and fiscal-intermediary game effectively can cost a practice thousands of dollars per year. What is the game? The payers make the claims process so complicated that even skilled medical office personnel make mistakes and each filing error presents the payer with an opportunity to reject a claim. At the very least the delayed payment of claims benefits the cashflow of the payer at the expense of the service provider, the latter effectively and unwittingly performing the function of a bank that has loaned money, interest free. More often than providers care to admit, as a result of a clerk's lack of persistence, many rejected claims are never re-submitted and are eventually written off. The result is game, set and match in favor of the payer.

CHAPTER 5

PROVIDER COMPENSATION

If our intent is to design a health care delivery system that operates as a free market, how we elect to compensate providers becomes pivotal. We have three compensation methodologies from which to choose. Recall that the proposed system's logic begins with the premise that health care is a public good to be provided to all Americans. This means that the revenue will come from tax dollars and not directly from the pockets of patients and/or their employers. How this will work and how tax revenue for the National Health Care Plan will be collected will be revealed in a later chapter.

Fee For Service Option

The first option is a fee-for-service system, a method with which we are all familiar. The Canadian health care system offers an excellent example. The Canadian physician bills the government for the care given and the provider will determine the specific treatments in each instance.

We reject this approach for the reasons we have previously discussed, as we do not wish to recreate the problems of our existing delivery system. It is also noteworthy that this FFS approach is one of the sources of dissatisfaction for Canadians, who otherwise seem to be generally proud of their plan (Armstrong et al, 1998).

At the top of our list of objections is that the interests of the physician and the patient may conflict. This is manifested by incentives that encourage over-treatment (Wong, 1998; Weiss, 1995). The sicker the patient, the more billing opportunities exist. It is true in any business venue that energy will be channeled to activity that produces the most revenue because that is the way we have constructed the incentives. Physicians will act no differently than any other businessperson, as our experience illustrates. In theory, if all Americans were suddenly to become well, health care would experience a financial crisis of galactic proportions.

According to conventional wisdom a fee-for-service system would appear to be the best choice if our objective is to create a free market health system. Can we not characterize the free market as a fee-for-service system? As we discussed in an earlier chapter, however, in health care all of the criteria of a free market system are not met. The recipient or user of the service does not pay the total cost of care and does not pay it directly. Fee for service is a transaction driven system and the recipient of care has insufficient knowledge to choose the appropriate service or to assess its quality. Without these key ingredients a free market cannot exist.

Physician As Employee

A second method of paying providers for the care they dispense is to make all providers employees of a public health service and pay them a salary for the work they do. What we have seen in other public health environments is a level of care that often fails to rise above mediocrity and a bureaucracy that, at its best, is tedious. At its worst the bureaucracy is unfathomable. That she was advocating a health care system governed by the church does not negate the sentiment expressed when Dr. Aleita Eck writes *"Government health care programs are often top-heavy, poorly responsive to real needs, easily abused, and wasteful – and the taxpayers are paying dearly... ."* (Eck, 1998).

Large, private medical business entities offer ample evidence that in spite of their aggressive efforts to insure both efficiency and effectiveness, it can be difficult to adequately incent salaried physicians to practice cost-effective medicine. Many physicians are self-motivated to perform and these are not the problem. Others are content to put in their time and take their paycheck. One practice with which the author was familiar placed a new, salaried physician in a brand new office in what was considered to be an under-served community. When this group's management became concerned that the growth in daily patient encounters had hit a plateau earlier than anticipated, they discovered that the physician had instructed schedulers to limit the number of patients per day to a level with which he was comfortable. In this instance the result was one in which patients were turned away. Would we expect a government health service to be any more successful in achieving cost-effectiveness?

Prepaid Health Care - Capitation

The third alternative is the full risk capitation arrangement utilized in some HMO industry models, an approach that has stirred much controversy.

Just because an effort fails, however, does not mean it was a bad idea and many great ideas throughout history have been successfully implemented only after numerous failures. The reasons for the failure of an idea are many and include poor timing, inadequate resources, planting the idea in infertile soil, misapplication of the idea, or sometimes just from a job poorly done. It is our contention that the reasons for the early failures of a full-risk capitation plan are many and that all of the above were contributing factors to some degree.

The National Health Care Plan that will be unveiled in the next chapter will rely on a full-risk capitation concept.

This is a point where the reader is asked to withhold judgment. Many are thinking, as they read these words, "it's just another HMO program. It will never work."

Our proposal does, indeed, borrow from the HMO concept, just as it borrows from business and industry. If the reader can keep an open mind he or she will see that this capitation plan is something very different.

The objectives of the prepaid concept in managed care were noble.

- Reward providers for maintaining the health of their patients and offer incentives to encourage health prevention and education.
- Place physicians in a position from which they can control utilization.
- Provide incentives to encourage exploration of new, more cost-effective treatment protocols and to utilize non-institutional care to a greater degree.
- Minimize the paperwork.
- Simplify the health care delivery process.

None of these were bad ideas and in some of these things managed care has been successful. The utilization of out-patient surgical centers, after-hours care, and home health care are just a few examples where prepaid health has had a positive impact on both the quality and the cost of care.

Some critics of managed care cite the growing list of the uninsured as further evidence of the failure of the HMO. We remind the reader, however, that providing universal coverage to all Americans was never an objective of the HMO movement any more than it has been the objective of the private insurance system.

Providing universal coverage to all Americans is, however, the primary objective of the health care plan we are proposing. We also want to make it clear to the reader that the plan we are about to unveil is not another HMO, in fact this plan eliminates all insurers, including managed care companies, from the health care delivery system. They simply will not exist.

The ideas we have borrowed from the HMO movement were good ones – there were many ideas that were not good – and, we have engineered a structure in which they will produce positive results. The logic begins with the concept that the incentives in a full-risk capitation approach reward the physicians, not for procedures but for the health of the patient. Our objective is to create a scenario in which the interests of the patient – their good health - parallel the interests of the provider and we can accomplish this by creating a direct relationship between the health of the patients and the financial health of a physician's practice.

A predictable objection to our prepaid health plan is that the HMO industry exhibited many examples where providers were even more likely to make decisions on the basis of there own self-interest than were physicians in a FFS environment. Antagonists will remind us that some physicians will abuse the process and deny patients the treatments they need in the interests of meeting their own financial objectives.

We would not begin to argue that some physicians will do exactly that, just as some physicians in the FFS environment will administer unnecessary tests, perform unnecessary surgeries, or defraud Medicare in the interest of meeting their financial objectives. Physicians are imperfect human beings and there is no system so perfect that it can prevent abuse by the self-serving.

In the business world, however, it is a universally accepted axiom that the financially successful business is one that focuses on the needs of its customers, even when it means forgoing short-term rewards in exchange for long-term benefits. As well as this is understood in the business community, there are still many business men and women who will sacrifice long-term customer satisfaction for short-term financial returns. Some get away with it, but more often than not, businesses lose customers and risk losing their business as a result. The enterprise that attends to the customer's needs first will be successful over the long term far more often than those that do not.

In our existing health care system no such consequences exist. It will be our intent, in this new system of health delivery, to create the same type of environment, one in which the practitioners who put the interests of their patients first will be more successful than those who focus on their own interests.

In our present HMO environment this power is absent because in the majority of instances, it is the employer who, once a year can review the contract and make changes. And, although the employer will certainly be influenced by the level of satisfaction expressed by its employees, the cost of coverage will have far more leverage in the decision-making process.

There were many defects in design that contributed to the poor execution of prepaid care in the managed care environment. We suggest that these defects can be remedied.

Probably the most consequential flaw was that the revenues have never been sufficient to allow the prepaid system to work properly (Morrison, 2000). The intent was that there would be sufficient funds for the primary care physician to care for his patient population and also enjoy a healthy business in the process. The reality was an environment where it was difficult for the provider to be financially successful. Because the capitation revenue was never adequate and had to be shared between the managed care enterprise and the provider, the physician's business was only marginally healthy when his patients were healthy. If a patient became seriously ill or suffered severe injury the physician's financial health suffered proportionately.

If the prepaid approach is to work the physician must generate sufficient resources to care for his patients who are seriously ill. What we want is a system where the physician has sufficient resources to provide the care and treatment his patients require, and where he enjoys surplus revenue when his patients are healthy. As you will see shortly, there is more than enough money spent on health care in the

United States to provide such an environment, especially when the third parties are cut out of the equation. Once the revenue is adequate to achieve these objectives, aggregate cost – the only cost that matters – can be controlled by allowing it to keep pace with inflation, not out-pace it.

The second design flaw was that the utilization standards in the HMO environment were established by the managed care company and the doctor was often as frustrated as the patient with regard to what the plan would cover and what it would not. Physicians are rarely comfortable when they are told what kind of medicine to practice. It is a whole different matter to live under rules established by some external power, one that has little if any direct contact with patients, than it is to live under rules of one's own making in a setting in which one is not only accountable to one's patients but must discuss treatment decisions face to face.

The third flaw was that the patients had little recourse when they were dissatisfied with either the physician or the managed care enterprise. Besides the fact that it is always difficult to pin down responsibility, the patient had limited ability to change physicians and virtually no ability to change managed-care companies. In a system where the decision to change physicians is the sole province of the patient, things will be very different.

A fourth flaw is that many of the primary care physicians involved in prepaid care simultaneously practiced FFS medicine (Shortell, 2000). The practice of medicine is challenging enough under one venue. Divide a practice into one segment for FFS and another for managed care and you have raised the complexity level significantly. Most disconcerting was the resulting duality of standards; FFS patients get one level of care, HMO patients get another.

Each of these flaws can be eliminated in a well-designed and well-engineered system, constructed on a logical premise, and managed consistent with that logic. The result is a plan that merges the interests of patients and providers and it is just such a plan that we offer.

Mel Hawkins

A fifty-four year old woman visiting family in another city experienced what was believed to be a stroke. The physician on duty at the urgent care facility where the patient was initially taken called for an ambulance. The patient was transported to the emergency room of a local hospital and by the time of her arrival her symptoms of numbness, partial paralysis on the right side of her body, and loss of speech had begun to abate.

Although pleased with the patient's slowly improving condition the attending emergency room physician was inclined to risk neither the health of her patient, nor her own liability and that of the hospital. The doctor administered the standard dosage of aspirin and ordered the full protocol of diagnostics including, blood work, chest x-rays and a CAT scan. By the time the normal findings of both the x-rays and CAT scan were reported the patient's speech and motor skills had returned. She was, nevertheless, sent upstairs for observation under a 23-hour admission and additional lab work was ordered.

By the next day it would have been difficult to tell that the patient had been ill and the episode was diagnosed as an atypical migraine. The woman was discharged with instructions to follow-up with her family physician upon her return home. After two office calls with her family physician, an MRI, sonogram, echogram, a second CAT scan, interpretations by a neurologist, radiologist and pathologist, the diagnosis of atypical migraine was again the consensus. Fortunately the woman and her husband had good health coverage. The amount for which they were responsible was limited to two $15.00 copays, her $350 deductible, the $1,250 out-of-pocket limit and one $20.00 prescription. Imagine the impact for a family with little or no health insurance?

CHAPTER 6

HEALTH CARE AS AN ECONOMIC SYSTEM

Before we can unveil a new plan we must delve a little deeper into the economics of health care to better understand what must change and why.

Much of the complexity of our current health care system, and our inability to find meaningful and workable solutions, stem from our misconceptions of health care viewed as an economic system. The literature is replete with references to concerns about the undesirable influence of the profit motive on insurers, managed care organizations and providers (Makover, 1998; Shi and Singh, 2000; Dranove, 2000; Armstrong, 1998). So also are references to the assertion that the forces of the free-market economy are a major contributor to the problems of modern health care and also obstruct reform efforts.

The reader should have no illusions. Health care is an economic system, one influenced by economic forces, but not in the manner alleged. One of the ways health care differs from a consumer market is that health care has been stretched, pulled, patched and modified relentlessly for the better part of the twentieth century. Like a software package, poorly understood by second-generation programmers responding to user complaints and change requests, health care has been altered beyond the point of recognition. What remains is a bastardized system of logic that simply does not function in the manner in which it was originally designed. At the same time the expectations of the user, both the American people and health care providers, have not been adjusted to factor in these many changes and modifications.

Earlier we compared health care to a retail market and concluded that the system's structure no longer fits the model of a consumer-market. In this chapter we will take a more in-depth look at health care as an economic model to discover how things actually work and to learn how its structure can be re-engineered.

Mel Hawkins

The Elements of a Free Market

An economic free market consists of buyers and sellers. Sellers attempt to discover the needs and wants of buyers and, on the basis of their understanding of these needs, sellers invest their limited capital resources in the production of goods and services they believe will fulfill those needs and for which buyers will be willing to pay. A seller has no guarantees that his investments will be rewarded and the investment is, therefore, considered to be at risk.

If the seller has succeeded in identifying a true need the customer will be willing to exchange something of value (cash) for the seller's goods and services. The more completely these products and services fulfill the buyer's need, the more value that buyer is willing to offer in exchange. It is the buyer's perception or judgment of the value of the seller's products that drives demand. The more the product is valued and the greater the number of customers who value it, the more those customers will be willing to pay to acquire the product and, as a result, the greater the seller's return on his investment.

If the seller has misjudged the buyer's need, he will sell little or no product and his investment will not be recovered, resulting in an economic loss. If the seller's products satisfy a portion of the buyer's need the seller may sell part of his merchandise, but may need to discount the price in order to do so.

Success goes to the seller who most effectively and consistently meets the needs of his customers, but even he dare not be complacent. A marketplace is a dynamic environment and a customer's needs undergo continuous change. Sellers of goods and services must not only adapt to these changing customer requirements but they must also compete with other sellers on price, quality and value, for a share of a finite market.

For the marketplace to function the buyer must be knowledgeable, meaning he knows what he wants and how much it is worth to him; he must be willing, meaning he is free to purchase or not; and he must have the means. Absent any of these criteria, the market is not a "free" market.

Free markets are self-regulating in the sense that they gravitate toward equilibrium between supply and demand. Supply and demand are the forces that drive the system. The cycle always begins with a customer need – demand – and this demand is in a constant state of

72

flux. The market exists only as long as there are sellers willing to risk their capital to meet the needs of the customer. Sellers who are unable to earn a return on their investment are quickly eliminated from the competition. Free markets have zero tolerance for both ineffectiveness – the inability to respond to the needs of the customer – and inefficiency – the inability to do so at a profit.

The Role of Profits

Profits play a vital role in a free market. The term profit is just another name for "return on investment." It is the prospect of a return on investment that leads a seller to the decision to place his capital at risk. Profits keep the seller healthy, willing, and able to re-invest his capital all over again. Absent a return on his investment to replenish his capital assets, a seller would lose his ability to reinvest, even if he were willing. The term nourishment effectively describes the role profits play in a free market.

Without nourishment one cannot survive and the same is true of markets, but profits are more than just the food of business. Just as human beings derive more satisfaction from a good meal than satiation of one's hunger, there is an intrinsic pleasure or sense of accomplishment in the quest for profits. Both the nourishment and the intrinsic pleasure attached to the process of generating a profit provide an incentive to the entrepreneur. It is a rare businessman who does not delight in the praise of a happy customer.

As with any seller in a free market the businessman must be focused on the needs of his customers. To paraphrase respected business and organizational management guru, Peter Drucker, successful business organizations don't make money, they satisfy customers (Drucker, 1974). This simple yet sage advice is often difficult for even experienced business professionals to comprehend. Some will argue that they are in business to make money. While it is true the decision to enter into business is motivated by a desire for a return on one's capital – and also that we cannot remain in business unless we earn such a return – once we are in business we get paid only when customers are satisfied with our product or service. Think of business as a game. The object of the game is to satisfy customers (put the ball in the basket). Profits (points) are the way the game is scored.

The successful businessman strives to understand his customer's needs and expectations, knowing that such understanding is key to success. One of our objectives in re-engineering our health care system as an economic market is to create such understanding.

The fable of goose and golden egg also illustrates this point well. Our motivation might be to harvest golden eggs, but we won't collect many golden eggs if all we do is squeeze the goose. Our success is contingent upon our ability to keep the goose healthy and satisfied and our reward is a stream of golden eggs. The financial reward of the practice of medicine is the stream of revenue generated by a practice full of healthy and satisfied patients. Oddly enough the intrinsic rewards of the practice of medicine also flows from a practice full of healthy and satisfied patients. One could say the successful practice of medicine, much like any successful business venture, can best be achieved when the interests of both the patient (customer) and provider (seller) are parallel.

What we discover is that the problem with the American health care system is not the result of the influence of profits, but just the opposite. Problems exist because, as a result of all the reforms and short-sighted fixes of the last fifty years, market forces are unable to effectively influence profits. What is missing is the pressure to be profitable in a competitive marketplace where quality and cost-effectiveness are rewarded and where poor quality and inefficiency suffer consequences. The problems are aggravated because our misinterpretation of the role of profits diverts our attention from the root causes and makes meaningful solutions that much more difficult to find. Instead we repeatedly make the same mistake.

The Armstrongs, writing of the Canadian system, illustrate this misinterpretation for us. They credit the not-for-profit status of the Canadian system for helping keep cost down. They suggest that:

1. A share of expenditures goes to profit and they allude to examples where insurance, managed care and pharmaceutical companies report huge profits and offer rich compensation packages to their executive staff.

2. Competition, they say, encourages investment in expensive technologies designed to attract customers. Competition also means marketing and its associated costs. They cite the high cost of brand name drugs, compared with generic equivalents.

Later they write:

Huge corporations are the driving force of health care in the United States. They act in their own best interests by squeezing maximum profits out of illness and injury and by devoting massive resources to influencing government to allow the private sector to continue to maximize profits. However the overall social consequences of "free enterprise in health care are the tendency toward monopolistic control on the one hand, and on the other the restriction of access to care for tens of millions of "unprofitable" Americans who are either shunted onto public-sector programs or simply excluded altogether. (Armstrong, 1998).

These assessments are based, we believe, on a misinterpretation of the role of economics in health care. Let's examine each of their observations in turn.

Corporations: Insurance and Managed Care

The Armstrongs are correct that insurance and managed care entities siphon great sums of money out of the health care system and also that these entities contribute to the restricted access to care for millions of Americans. It is also correct that these organizations exert disproportionate influence on the system and on the political process. So how are the Armstrongs and others wrong? It is a lack of recognition that the system's problems result from the logical framework of the system and not with profits. Once again we suggest that **the problem is not that these organizations generate profits, it is that they exist at all**. Health care is like an automobile engine with the timing belt incorrectly set. The engine runs, but not as it was intended.

The question we should be asking, subsequent to our acknowledgment that health care is a public good, is what value do large insurance, managed care and other "non-provider" organizations contribute to the system? The system suffers because of the logical inefficiency of spending such enormous sums on non-value-added activities that contribute little or nothing to the direct care of patients.

These organizations would create inefficiency and redundancy even when operating as non-profit entities.

Competition and Technology

The role of competition and technology are similarly misunderstood and offer further evidence that even intelligent people can forget some of the most basic truths about a free-market system and the vital role of profits.

Again the Armstrong's offer an illustration: *"Competition creates duplication of expensive technologies in health care, not cost-effectiveness"* (Armstrong, 1998). We submit that just the opposite is true. Competition does not create inefficiency; competition in a free market always leads us toward efficiency and a toward a balance between supply and demand, neither of which is ever fully attained. (McGuire, 1999)

It is our assertion that the problems of health care are the result of a disconnection between supply and demand and not the progeny of a competitive marketplace or investment in expensive technologies. Manufacturing offers numerous examples.

Executives of an assembly plant elect to invest capital in new assembly technology. The expectation is that the new technology will increase production capacity, reduce unit cost of goods produced and improve quality. Assuming these expectations are realized, once the technology is operational, the plant's ability to compete for market share is significantly enhanced. The reward for improving the quality and cost of a customer's product is new business from existing customers and sales to new customers. The entrepreneur is trying to respond to an anticipated demand – a customer need and expectation. In the end the investor is either rewarded or penalized, not by a public or private regulatory agency, but by the marketplace. It is the risk of a financial loss that inhibits investors from sinking capital in products that make poor business sense.

Competition is an essential ingredient without which free markets would inexorably fail. Producers of goods and services compete for market share. Whether an assembly operation, a movie theater chain or some other service provider, producers must distinguish their products and services from their competition. Profits are the reward that flows to those who, through their creative energy, best satisfy the customers for whom they compete. Striving to gain this competitive advantage is what drives excellence.

However much we might wish to believe that human beings consistently produce excellence without incentives, evidence would suggest it just isn't so. How many times do we, in fact, see degradation in both product or service quality, and also in innovation, when there are no competitors challenging us to raise our standards and no incentives to reward our performance. We find over and over that only a few such things occur out of altruism.

In the United States we regulate those industries where there are too few producers to achieve a competitive marketplace. The purpose of the regulation is to create, artificially, the same results in terms of price and quality that competition would provide naturally in a free market economy.

The Canadian system has accomplished one thing the United States has not and that is the recognition of health care as a public good. Canada has chosen to distribute this public good through a government-regulated system. Neither will be perfect, but we will predict with some confidence that Canada will always lag behind the United States in quality and innovation.

Another misconception is the frequently touted assumption that rising costs are inherently bad. In every economic venue in our country costs rise and health care will be no exception, whether operating as a free market or as a regulated industry. What distinguishes a healthy economy from one not so healthy is that in the former, productivity and value rise at a rate faster than the rate of increased costs. If value rises at an equal or faster rate than cost, then the rising cost of production can be viewed as a good thing as each dollar spent purchases more value than the previous dollar. Flat or diminishing revenues, for any length of time, results in a stagnant system.

Think of any government program and compare it to the free market. Costs rise in both venues, but in the government program costs seem always to rise at a faster rate than value and sometimes value does not increase at all. In a free market when the value of a product or service diminishes, customers abandon the product and the entity either fails or adapts. Government programs, on the other hand, disappear only when officials make a conscious decision to terminate. So pervasive is the problem that the enabling legislation of many state and federal programs contains a "sunshine" provision to guarantee that a program is not perpetuated without periodic assessment of its value.

Our challenge, after establishing health care as a public good, is not to increase the amount of regulation but to return health care to the venue of a free market economy. Naysayers may say this is not possible; that the two are incompatible, but recall that one of the ground rules established in the first chapter is that anything man can imagine, man can do.

The health care system proposed here has been designed to exist in two marketplaces, each of which will function in the broad free market economy, just as do hundreds of other micro-markets. The first market is a "simulated free market" and the second is a true free market. The two micro-markets will operate in tandem much as a supply chain in other industries. Both markets will have sellers who will place their capital at risk and will offer products and services to knowledgeable, willing and able buyers. Within each of these markets sellers will then be challenged to gain a competitive advantage and buyers will reward those providers who offer the best quality and the most innovation. Providers who cannot successfully compete for their share of the market will be forced to either exit the market altogether or, reinvent their product or service offering.

Primary Care Physicians Compete for Patients

The first market is a simulated market, one in which primary care physicians compete with other PCPs for patients. In our proposal, by virtue of our decision that health care is a public good, the public will pay for the care of all Americans through a capitation system. The market is described as "simulated," as price will be regulated in that capitation rates will be determined external to the market, but as we shall see, this does not alter the market's functionality. Because each American carries with them a stream of capitation revenue, all prospective patient/customers will possess the means. In addition to no restrictions on ability to pay, these patients will be free to choose any PCP in the market place. They are restricted neither by the type of coverage selected by their employer nor by limitations imposed by insurance, managed care or by any other organization.

While it is true that few Americans are in a position to assess the medical capabilities of their physician, there are many other criteria that contribute to the level of trust and confidence patients place in their doctor. In their search for a primary care physician a patient will look for those "product characteristics" that best meet their needs. No doubt convenience of location will be a factor as will the provider's reputation within the marketplace. A decision will also be based on a number of other criteria such as the attractiveness of the PCP's office, the friendliness of both the physician and his staff, and the hospitals to which the PCP admits. The panel of specialists to whom the PCP refers may also influence the patient's choices, as will the types of care the PCP will relegate to specialists. A woman of childbearing age, for example, may base her choice on how a PCP handles obstetrical care. Some patients will want a specialist handling their pregnancy and delivery while others will be content to rely on their family doctor.

When the patient selects their primary care physician they will pay for his services with the revenue stream dictated by their capitation rate just as consumers in the broader market pay for products and services with money they have earned. How the customer acquired his money does not influence the market's function. In order to have a successful medical practice, both clinically and fiscally; the PCP must be able to attract enough patients to generate the revenue necessary to cover his cost of doing business, including a healthy profit. The PCP's success is not assured, however, solely because a certain number of patients select him as their doctor. The PCP must also deliver a level of care that is judged to be acceptable by their patient population lest those patients leave dissatisfied, in search of another primary care physician.

As all patients and their health needs are unique, maintaining patient satisfaction requires flexibility and the primary care physician must be able to adjust his service offering according to the ever-changing expectations of his patients, no different that any other producer of goods and services. This seemingly subtle difference in the importance of physician/patient relationships leads to an enormous change in the way medicine is practiced.

Recall in an earlier section, we described the FFS system as transaction driven. This new market is relationship driven and the patient is more than capable of judging the quality of the relationship.

Mel Hawkins

The more effort the physician puts into the relationship the more successful he will be. A relationship in which the patient is a party to medical decisions and bears some responsibility for his own health is the ideal. Relationships have suffered in the minds of many who would tell you that there are some physicians that do an incredibly poor job of listening to their patients and giving the patient's point of view serious consideration. As patients across this nation will attest there are physicians who treat their patients like a commodity, devoting their energy and the energy of their practice staff to churning – getting as many patients through the process as possible, with as many billable services as possible.

As we have noted, this phenomena is not the result of bad, uncaring doctors, it is a consequence of health care as a billing game. Let us repeat. The system we propose irrevocably changes the game to one where the financial success of the practice, which is a function of the number of patients the practice is able to attract and retain, is largely determined by the level of satisfaction the patient has with the doctor/patient relationship.

We are not suggesting that patient satisfaction plays no role in American health care today, because many patients are free and do exercise their right to terminate their relationship with a physician with whom they are dissatisfied. At the same time there are many who are not free or whose freedom is restricted in some way. These restrictions, coupled with the inconvenience intrinsic in a decision to change doctors, limit the number of patients who exercise their right to choose. It is sad, but also true, that many Americans have become so desensitized because of the absence of a personal relationship with their physician, that such a relationship is no longer an expectation. The result is an ever-widening gap between patient and doctor, a gap that is in the best interests of neither.

Some patients also feel powerless to influence the quality of care they receive in the current system. Customer/buyers in a free market are never powerless. In the National Health Care Plan patients have a great deal of power to choose. The better a patient feels about his relationship with a doctor; the more he feels his physician listens, and the more time the physician takes to sell the treatment plan to the patient, the more trust and faith the patient will be likely to extend to his doctor. The physician was, a long time ago, a learned and trusted friend and we would all feel better about the care we receive if we could somehow restore the physician to this status. It is not our intent, however, to elevate the physician to a higher pedestal. **If we have a good relationship with our doctor we will be much more likely to view him or her as an imperfect human being striving to be the best possible practitioner of an uncertain science**.

In a conversation on the subject of the practice of medicine I once heard a trial judge comment that doctors have ascended to such a "god-like" stature it should not be surprising that people expect their physicians to be gods. The implication was that adverse outcomes are naturally viewed as the result of someone's screw up. While physicians do "screw up," they do so not nearly as often as we might think. Very often, even the best care and the most sophisticated procedures fail to produce the desired outcome. There is only so much medicine can do. Humans, it seems, are much more forgiving of another human being trying their best to do a difficult job, than of a god who fails us. The more the physician works to have a relationship with his patients the more likely those patients are to think of him as human.

To summarize this first marketplace we have physicians willing to invest their capital resources to offer primary care services to a large population of knowledgeable, willing and able patient/customer/buyers. In this market we define "knowledgeable" as knowing how one wants to be treated and how much one values care that is convenient, satisfying and comforting. What the physician offers is his professional expertise dedicated to the purpose of preserving and restoring the patient's health. In making the decision to offer his services the physician will need to approach his practice as both an artist of a very special craft and as a businessman.

The creation of this first free market will return health care to a place where physicians are no longer trapped in a competition that can only be won by playing a zero-sum game in which there are both winners and losers. The practice of medicine will, once more, be an endeavor in which physicians are rewarded for keeping their patients healthy and where, when good health is not achievable, patients are satisfied their doctor did his best to administer to their needs.

Mel Hawkins

The Marketplace of Specialized, Institutional and Ancillary Services

The second market to be established by this National Health Care Plan is a true free market, one in which sellers invest their capital and compete to provide specialized, institutional or ancillary medical services to knowledgeable, willing and able buyers. The sellers are physicians in a subspecialty practice; they are hospitals, laboratories, imaging centers, home health agencies and other ancillary providers. The buyer/customers are primary care physicians engaged in preserving and restoring the health of their patient population.

The sellers in this marketplace, like sellers in any market, must be able to find economic justification for their investment decisions. Where the investments are not justified the free-market system will penalize poor performance and service and will weed out low quality care. In other words, demand and quality will drive these investment/ business decisions, all of which will be at the investor's risk. The result is that those who succeed in satisfying their customer's needs and expectations will be rewarded with customers willing to pay a fair price. As we discussed earlier, the primary care physician's financial interest will best be served by the health of their patient population. The importance of quality care to the health of the PCPs practice will provide a powerful incentive for the primary care physician to choose the best subcontractors and, as a result, this marketplace will function in response to market forces, just as is the case in the broader marketplace. Once more we learn that in a free market nothing maintains the price/quality ratio better than the discriminating consumer. What is unique about health care, at least with respect to medical issues, is this role, the discerning consumer, can only be effectively played by the physician. In this instance, the primary care physician.

As with their primary care counterparts, specialty providers will no longer be trapped in a game where the only way to win is to maximize billable services that must then be submitted in conformance with a complicated set of criteria, seemingly disconnected from the care of the patients. The specialist's financial success will come instead, when they satisfy their customers. In this market, satisfaction is determined by how effectively the specialist teams with the primary care physician in support of the PCP's efforts

82

to attend to the needs of his patients. Success will come from the provision of quality care, at a competitive price. This market is both transaction and relationship driven.

In this market, price is not a given. It will fluctuate with the ebbs and tides of supply and demand. The better a seller can distinguish his services from the competition the more he can charge for his services. The relationship between the seller and customer in this market will be virtually identical to that between an OEM (original equipment manufacturer) and its suppliers. The seller is compensated for helping his customers take care of their customers.

Relationship, teamwork and innovation are vital in a setting in which a knowledgeable professional is himself held accountable and where he holds his team accountable. Add the active participation of the patient, who also bears responsibility for his own health, and we have a team of people each of whom bring their own expertise and perspective, working to provide a coordinated health plan.

There are no restrictions with regard to the primary care physician's choice of subcontractors other than those the PCP himself establishes. No insurance company or managed care organization will exist to establish approved listings of providers. The PCP must make his own choices and these will be made on the basis of price and on performance criteria where the latter is judged on two levels. The first is the PCP's comfort level with the credentials, skills and competency of the providers with whom he contracts and the second is whether these subcontractors help satisfy the PCP's patient/customer. The expectation will be that the subcontractor is a team player.

Economic forces will drive price, quality, continuous improvement and innovation and, as is true of all free markets, the forces of supply and demand seek equilibrium. Providers who are unable to satisfy their customer, the PCP, will be challenged to either re-engineer their product offering or go out of business.

A man in his mid-fifties had worked for a not-for-profit agency in an administrative role for two years. His prior job had been in middle management in a local bank. After many years he left the bank as a victim of an acquisition and consolidation, during which his position had been eliminated. The time between jobs had approached three years. At the bank he had been eligible for excellent benefits, including a generous health insurance package.

During his long lay-off the man's wife, also in her mid fifties, had developed some chronic health problems requiring ongoing medical care. As a result of her condition, she was limited in her ability to work. The couple had considered themselves fortunate when the husband found the job at the not-for-profit agency and they learned the agency offered health coverage. During the intervening period, access to health care had been difficult. The new health coverage was not as comprehensive as that which he had enjoyed at the bank, but it was a blessing even with riders for the woman's pre-existing health problems.

As is not uncommon in not-for-profit agencies, funding declined and once again, the man found himself unemployed. Unfortunately during the several seeks prior to this most recent job loss, the severity of his wife's illness had increased and the loss of coverage could not have come at a worse time. Thanks to the COBRA requirements, the couple was able to temporarily extend their health coverage, but at a cost of over $500 per month. For a couple with no income other than his unemployment compensation, and no immediate prospects, there was a limit to how long they would be able to afford coverage.

As a result of their misfortune, this well-educated, hard working, middle-class couple had slipped into the cracks of the American health care system.

CHAPTER 7

THE NATIONAL HEALTH CARE PLAN

In this section we will lay out the structure and mechanics of a health care plan, one that represents a dramatic but achievable alternative and which will guarantee health care for all Americans. This alternative uses the existing provider system but changes the rules of the game so they work for, rather than at cross purposes with, the benefit of the American people. This National Health Care Plan (NHCP) works because it corrects the basic flaws of the current health care system. It:

1. Establishes health care as a public good to be extended to all American citizens and legal aliens.
2. Retains the existing provider system of private practicing physicians and returns control of medical decision making to the physician.
3. Eliminates all non-value added activity and obviates the need for insurance, managed care, third-party payer, fiscal intermediary and the Centers for Medicare and Medicaid Services (Formerly the Health Care Finance Administration).
4. Creates a free market system made up of sellers and buyers. This system rewards sellers with profits for satisfying their customers and, in the process merges the interests of providers and patients.
5. Reallocates the billions of dollars spent on non-value-added activity to pay for care for those not covered under the current system and brings the growth of aggregate costs under control.

The assumptions upon which the system is constructed are:
- Health care is a basic right of citizenship
- If we have the best providers in the world we must endeavor to take good care of them.
- For a system to work we must place our faith in someone and we elect to place our faith in our physicians.

- It is okay for providers to make a profit. Profits are not bad, even for physicians. Critics of the existing system spend too much time lamenting their erroneous judgment that doctors and other providers are corrupted by an insatiable desire for profits. What we need is a system in which providers are rewarded for taking good care of their patients.
- Abuses of this or any system are inevitable. Rather than implement costly systems in a hopeless attempt to place controls at the end of the process, we provide internal controls in the form of incentives that reward excellence. Abuses, when identified, will require sanctions.
- The more we can minimize the role of government in health care, the better.

Our purpose in this section is to give the reader an easy overview of the plan and how it will work. In the chapters that follow we will delve into the details. We will compare the economics of this new system with that within which we now live. We will strive to show how the plan is likely to impact all of the actors in the health care drama, whether patients, providers or institutions. Finally we will attempt to address the questions, challenges and concerns of all parties, to the extent they can be anticipated.

The National Health Care Plan

The system we propose is simple, conceptually. Each primary care physician licensed to practice medicine in the United States will become a member of the "Primary Care Provider Panel" of the National Health Care Plan (NHCP). Responsibility for managing the health of patients will be delegated to the primary care physician (PCP) of the patient's choice.

Under the NHCP the Primary Care Physician (PCP) is accountable only to the patient and will function in the role of both personal physician and case manager. Although the case manager role bears similarity to the "gatekeeper" function, one of the more controversial components of the HMO concept, the roles are significantly different, as the reader will soon see.

The designation of Primary Care Physician (PCP) will include:
- General Practitioners
- Family Physicians
- Pediatricians electing to provide primary care
- General Internists wishing to focus their practice on primary care
- OB-Gyns also opting to accept responsibility for the primary care of their patient population

Every citizen and legal alien in the United States, regardless of age, sex, race, religion or sexual preference will be eligible for complete coverage under the National Health Care Plan (NHCP). All they must do is register with a Primary Care Physician of their choosing, provided that PCP is open to additional patients. The status of a PCP's practice with regard to their willingness to accept new patients must be available to the public at all times. While a primary care physician's name is listed as accepting new patients she may not refuse a patient that selects her as a personal physician, absent reasonable cause. The integrity of this selection process is vital to the success of the plan.

An individual's social security number will be the identifying number as the patient's name is enrolled simultaneously on the database of the Primary Care Physician and of the federal agency designated to manage the enrollment information. The enrollment information will include a specific set of data on the patient to be delineated in a later paragraph.

We are proposing that the United States Census Bureau be designated as the agency responsible for the collection and maintenance of the enrollment data. Given that the responsibility for managing this enrollment information will also serve the Bureau's census function, the integration of these functions is expected to improve quality of the data and save tax dollars.

Each patient will receive an identification card with a magnetic strip to be scanned upon arrival at any point of medical service delivery in the United States. When scanned, any provider asked to deliver care and treatment of a patient will have access to all of the basic information necessary to initiate treatment including the name, contact information and tax identification number of the case manager who will be responsible for paying the cost of all covered services. The identification card may also contain information about allergies, blood type, special health conditions, organ donor information as well as other useful data. At some point in the future the use of thumb print, a tool more difficult to lose, or other sophisticated process might well replace the health care identification card.

By accepting the patient's enrollment the Primary Care Physician accepts full professional and financial responsibility for the total medical care of the patient. The care will include:

- Medical and surgical care
- Hospitalization and all inpatient services
- Emergency and after-hours "urgent" care including medically necessary ambulance services
- Immunizations
- Health Care education and prevention
- Diagnostic tests to include lab, x-ray, mammography, EKG, EEG, MRI, CAT scans and any other procedure selected for diagnostic purposes.
- Prosthetic devices
- Prescription Drugs
- Mental health care, whether outpatient or inpatient, and
- Long-term care.

Dental and optical coverage could also be provided by the National Health Care Plan but we have not addressed the specifics of this coverage other than to assume that, if these were covered, the primary care physician could elect to contract with providers of this care just as they would any other provider.

Any treatment or service the Primary Care Physician is unable to provide directly shall be provided at PCP's cost through contractual agreements with a specialty physician, hospital, clinic or ancillary provider of the PCP's choosing. As the purchaser of specialty, institutional and ancillary care, the PCP will be in a position to negotiate contracts with these providers that identify what services the PCP will purchase from the provider and at what price. These agreements place the sub-contracting providers in a position in which they must compete for the business of the PCPs in their community and be held accountable by the PCP for the quality of the care they provide. As we have noted, this introduction of a knowledgeable consumer satisfies a key element of an economic market in which supply and demand and other economic forces will come into play. It is an imperfect marketplace, of course, as are most markets in the real world, but it will function to keep prices down and quality up.

Referral or subcontracting with a specialist or other provider is not a passing of the responsibility for the patient's care. The PCP will retain financial and professional responsibility for the care of her patients at all times. Case management is the tool the PCP will use to fulfill this dual responsibility. Case management is not synonymous with "gate keeping" and is defined simply as the process of managing all care needed by a patient.

The gatekeeper in the HMO was responsible for exerting control over utilization, pursuant to both acceptable medical standards as well as the utilization standards established by the managed care entity. Upon approval of a referral to a specialist the gatekeeper would effectively turn the case over to her specialty colleague for the duration of the treatment to be provided by the specialist. Referrals were restricted to specialists approved or under contract to the managed care entity. The specialist was accountable to the managed care company for the quality of care provided. Although the gatekeeper would most likely want to be kept informed on a patient's progress, she would not typically play an active role in the patient's care until the patient was released from the specialist's care.

As case manager under the NHCP the primary care physician will be responsible for controlling utilization pursuant to acceptable medical standards and to utilization standards that she herself has established. When making a referral to a specialist the PCP will not be handing the patient off, rather, she will be asking for the specialist's assistance in the formulation and administration of a treatment plan. At no time will the case manager relinquish her role as the professional ultimately responsible for the patient's health and neither will the PCP's accountability to the patient be delegated.

It is envisioned that the primary care physician will ask her subcontractors to look at developing a treatment plan as a team responsibility. How willing a given specialist will be to accept this challenge will be a major influence in the PCP's process for selection of specialists and other providers.

Primary Care Physician Compensation

As compensation for accepting responsibility for the health of his patient population the PCP shall receive a monthly capitation payment for each patient listed on his panel. The capitation payment will be disbursed directly by the federal agency designated with this responsibility, to the primary care physician at the beginning of each month. The amount of the capitation will be actuarially determined on the basis of such criteria as the age and sex of the patient, taking into consideration any special medical circumstances that may exist.

Recalling that our objective is to assure coverage for every American, it is imperative that the capitation rates be fair and provide the primary care physician with sufficient revenue to provide adequately for his patient population and for his practice from a business point of view. **It will benefit no one if a capable and marketable physician is pulled into financial difficulty while trying to provide quality care to his patients.**

As we have suggested, under a current managed-care plan the reality has been that the PCP, or gatekeeper, receives barely enough cap revenue to enjoy a profitable practice and finds himself under financial duress when the patient has serious health care problems. Under the NHCP the primary care physician will receive capitation adequate to take care of the patient with serious illness or injury and still make a reasonable profit. While the patient is healthy the PCP will enjoy a higher profit. This arrangement creates the best case scenario in which there is an incentive for the PCP to use his best efforts to prevent illness and to maintain the patient's health. Concomitantly, the PCP will have adequate resources to provide whatever care the patient requires with no pressure to deny care solely on the basis of its cost.

This does not suggest that there is no incentive to keep costs under control. Cost control is still vital to the interests of physician's practice, to the patient and to the American public, the ultimate payer. Controlling cost and withholding care to save money are not at all the same activity.

Because adequate capitation is so vital to the success of the NHCP, the quality of the actuarial work becomes crucial. The greater the risks the patient's health presents the higher the capitation rates must be. For example, the capitation rate for care of healthy women of child-bearing age will likely be higher than that paid for the care of healthy young men and the rate for the elderly will be higher still. Capitation for patients with chronic medical problems such as diabetes and other diseases will also be higher just as the cost of providing care to these men and women is greater. A significant amount of work has been done by the managed care industry to develop actuarial standards and this work must continue to evolve.

Payment of the capitation at the beginning of every month eliminates much of the cash flow concerns of a primary care practice and it becomes the PCP's responsibility to marshal this cashflow prudently in order to staff, equip and supply his practice. He must also be in a position to purchase from the medical marketplace, prescription drugs and the other medical services his patients require.

By assigning this responsibility to the primary care physician we place a knowledgeable decision-maker of medical purchase transactions at the point of purchase, rather than in an insurance or HMO office several bureaucratic layers away. When the interests of the patient and the PCP are merged, better decisions are made whether viewed from a medical or fiscal perspective.

Where do we find the money to achieve the level of capitation revenue the NHCP envisions? The answer is, we use all of the money spent on health care in the current U.S. system and we only spend that money on direct care of patients. None of the cash will be expended to pay for insurance coverage and the other activities of the existing health care system unrelated to direct care.

For the sake of consistency all data is taken from the Census data for the year 1999. The 1999 Census was estimated at 272,691,000. Based upon estimated annual expenditures in 1999 for health services and supplies, excluding dental expenditures, of $1,133.1 Billion, the annual expenditure per citizen is about $4,155 (See Table 7.1). This

Table 7.1

1999 U. S. Health Care Expenditures per person
Excluding Dental Expenditures

	$ 1,133.10	Billion
Estimated U.S. Population for 1999**	272,691,000	
Expenditures per capita (Annual)	$ 4,155	
Expenditures per capita (Monthly)	$ 346	

* U.S. Census, Statistical Abstracts of the United States, Table No. 160

** U.S. Census, Statistical Abstracts of the United States, Table No. 2

amount, actuarially distributed to the entire primary care provider panel, will purchase comprehensive care for all Americans and will give the physician the resources needed to practice high quality medicine while maintaining a financially viable practice. This includes Americans in nursing homes and those with serious injuries and illnesses, both chronic and acute. During the initial year of the National Health Care Plan it must take into consideration the millions of men and women who, prior to the NHCP, have not had access to all of the care they required. The likelihood that these individuals will have unattended needs is great and the cost may also be great. This category of care will be given a special designation and will be referred to simply as "catch up" care. A portion of the total NHCP Tax Revenue will be allocated for this population.

We will save a detailed breakdown of the revenue issues, including how it will be collected, for later in this chapter.

One of the objectives of the National Health Care Plan is to provide comprehensive health care, universally to the American people with minimal involvement of state and federal government. While Americans are blessed with the best form of government in the world we also have little faith that government can work efficiently and cost-effectively outside of a narrow range of activities. It is our assertion that the health care system will be most effectively managed by health care professionals. The government will be called upon to provide only that support that can best be handled in a centralized manner.

At the federal level those few functions would be:

1. The maintenance of both a patient and provider census list as part of the overall Census function
2. Collection of tax revenue through a NHCP Payroll Tax
3. Distribution of funds to the primary care providers via monthly capitation payments according to a capitation-rate schedule. The cap schedule will be provided by an independent body to be convened expressly for this purpose.

The role of state government will also be limited. States will create, fund and monitor a medical review board to address the issues of licensing and grievances.

In the case of both state and federal government, minimizing the involvement of these levels of government will reduce the risk that bureaucracies, like cancers, will quickly grow out of control and, will siphon critical health care dollars away from the people who are responsible for providing care. **In the act of taking scarce resources away from providers we take "care" away from people**.

There will be no need for other governmental agencies, fiscal intermediaries or for private health insurance and managed-care companies as the functions these entities perform in our current health care system will no longer add value, if indeed that was ever the case. Government agencies can be shut down and private companies can reallocate their resources to respond to whatever business opportunities they can identify, possibly including re-insurance coverage for Primary Care Providers. Governments both state and federal, may need to provide assistance to help retrain displaced workers in either the public or private sector. Fortunately, these are typically well-educated Americans with marketable skills.

The independent body charged with the responsibility for setting captitation rates will include representation from the medical community but the majority of its members must be private citizens.

How this is structured can be determined at a later date, but the primary objective is that representation be as diverse and apolitical as possible.

The mission of this independent body will be to employ actuarial science from the private marketplace to set capitation rates on the basis of what is necessary to fairly compensate the medical community for the care it provides. Again we refer to our purpose. The objective of the NHCP is to assure that every American receives the care they require and that the cost of that care is born by the public. Cost controls are made part of the process as the PCP is rewarded for keeping costs at an optimal level. By optimum level we mean one that balances the medical and fiscal interests of all parties.

Annually this body will reconvene to review cap rates for the purpose of assessing the need for increases and other adjustments to the capitation schedules necessary to adapt to the dynamic world of medicine.

Although our objective is to adequately fund the plan we believe that this can be accomplished while reducing the aggregate health care expenditures for the U.S. Recall that a significant portion of the current health care expenditures go to people and organizations that are not directly involved in providing care to patients. Estimates vary, but it appears that as much as twenty-five percent of aggregate health care expenditures are absorbed by these "non-providers" (Armstrong 1998; Pricewaterhouse-Coopers 2001). We anticipate that the reallocation of this amount – twenty-five percent of current, aggregate health expenditures – will be sufficient to provide care to the fifteen percent of the population who currently lack health coverage.

During the first year we propose that one fifth of those funds (or five percent of the aggregate health care budget using 1999 data) to be allocated to citizens without prior coverage, be placed in a special fund labeled as the "catch-up care fund." Physicians will have an option of applying for a special designation for patients from this population, whose conditions meet special criteria during the first year. Thereafter the physician will assume full responsibility for a patient's care. It is not anticipated that the "Catch-up Care" provision will continue into the second year of the NHCP.

These funds will be dispersed through the re-insurance process, which will be discussed in a later section of this chapter.

Table 7.2

Allocation of Aggregate Health Care Funding
Excluding Dental Expenditures
(Shown in Billions)

	Total Funding*	Cap to MD	Catch Up Care
Year One	$ 1,133.1	$ 1,076.4	$ 56.7
Year Two	$ 1,133.1	$ 1,133.1	$ -

* U.S. Census, Statistical Abstract of the United States, Table No. 160

In the second year the full 100 percent of the aggregate budget will flow to Primary Care Physicians through capitation payments. This will, effectively, give PCP's better than a five percent increase in capitation revenue in the second year, without a corresponding increase in tax revenue. Thereafter, increases in the aggregate health care allotments will be made by the independent entity described above. A decision to increase capitation rates from year-to-year must be based on some objective criteria. It is recommended that the benchmark be the Consumer Price Index. Not, however, on only the medical component of the CPI, as has been the case in the past. This will enable physicians to cover increases in their own costs, only some of which are under the primary care physician's control.

Taxation and Revenue Issues

How we collect and distribute revenue will require changes in our tax structure at the federal level.

Capitation amounts due to the PCP on the basis of the patients who have selected them will be paid out of a National Health Care Fund. The tax revenue to support this program will be channeled into this dedicated fund. We do not want the program's funding jeopardized because health care must compete for fiscal support with other federal programs. We have all seen the Congress, when under political pressure, rob one program to pay for another. This would destroy one of the most critical components of the NHCP, that the primary care physician will be assured of adequate revenues to meet the needs of his patients while still allowing reasonable profits to reward the most capable practitioners.

Source and Collection of Revenue

We begin with the assumption that, in the current system, we already spend enough money on health care to provide quality care to every single American. What we must do is redirect the dollars that are already being spent into the National Health Care Fund from which capitation payments will be dispersed.

Currently the sources of money paid by individuals includes:
- Cash paid to providers for the care received
- Cash paid to insurance companies and managed care entities, including the portion deducted from an individuals pay check.
- Payroll taxes collected for Medicare
- Other tax dollars assessed by local, state and federal government that are designated for health care whether Medicaid or other programs
- Individual donations to not-for-profit health care agencies, facilities and providers

And from employers:
- Direct payments to providers on behalf of employees
- Employer portion of private health insurance and managed care premiums for their employees
- Employer portion of payroll taxes for Medicare
- Worker's compensation premiums
- Other tax dollars assessed by local, state and federal government that are designated for health care whether Medicaid or other programs
- Corporate contributions to not-for-profit agencies, facilities and providers

Every single dollar spent on health care emanates from individual taxpayers and their employers. We take our capitalist economy so much for granted that we sometimes forget that all revenue is generated by business and industry. Today these dollars must pass from individuals and their employers, through what is often a complicated route during which chunks, both large and small, are chipped away by a wide range of organizations that are funded by the health care system, but which provide no direct medical service to patients. These "non-providers" include:

- Insurers
- Managed care entities
- Federal, state and local government
- Third-party administrators
- Fiscal intermediaries
- Collections agencies
- Attorneys

Under the NHCP all funds for the purchase of health care will be collected through a NHCP Payroll Tax to be collected equally from individual employees and their employers. This revenue flow will totally and irrevocably bypass the non-providers.

The collection of taxes for any public program and at any level of government is always a sensitive issue. Most Americans understand that they must pay taxes, but few are happy with the amount of tax they must pay and no one delights in the obligation. What Americans citizens want is to see how they benefit from the taxes they pay, along with assurance that the taxes are being fairly assessed. Taxpayers typically want to know that their tax dollars are efficiently utilized in a way that creates real value for American citizens.

We believe that since every American will benefit from the health care provided through the National Health Care Plan, every American or legal alien with income, whether earned from work or from investments, should contribute to the NHCP Fund. We also believe that this taxation process should be as simple as possible.

What we propose is that the current Medicare Tax be replaced by the NHCP Payroll Tax. We also propose that this tax be assessed on all other Personal Income from interest and dividends at the same rate.

The actual amount of the tax will be determined at a later point in time. For purposes of this illustration we know that in 1999, the $1.133 trillion dollars spent annually for health care represents approximately 14.7 percent of total Personal Income for 1999. As this percentage will be shared equally by employer and employee, each will pay approximately 7.35 percent of the employees gross pay, to be collected in the same manner as the current Medicare tax. Currently 1.45 percent of gross payroll is already collected each from individuals and their employers through the Medicare Tax. To fund the National Health Care Plan we will simply increase the rate from 1.45 to 7.35 percent for employee and also for the employer and change the name of the Tax. The incremental change or additional tax for the payee in this illustration, whether individual or employer, will be 5.9 percent of the employee's income.

All new taxes have an impact on the taxpayer and no doubt some taxpayers will be adversely impacted by this NHCP Tax. Let's think about the impact across the whole population, however, and assess whether it is positive or negative.

Working individuals are currently paying some portion of their health care costs. For those who do not have health insurance coverage it is the cash paid to health care providers when they find it necessary to seek medical assistance. Many of the working but uninsured individuals and their families delay going to a doctor unless it is absolutely necessary. Individuals who have health coverage are currently paying all of the premium if they purchase coverage individually, or the employee share of the premium for coverage provided by an employer. Individuals also pay all out of pocket expenses, including deductibles, co-payments and co-insurance, as well as expenses for care that is not covered by their insurance. For many Americans the total amount paid for health care and health coverage, including the Medicare Taxes they pay, is significantly more than the estimated 7.35 percent of their gross pay and the possibility that costs will increase is ever-present.

These costs will no longer be the individual's responsibility, as their NHCP Tax will purchase comprehensive care for the individual and their dependents. For those who are now paying more than 7.35 percent, the NHCP plan will result in out-of-pocket savings as well as provide a guarantee of comprehensive health coverage.

For the working but uninsured this new tax in the amount of 7.35 percent of their pay will seem like a lot, until they step back and realize that these dollars pay for something they cannot now afford. The NHCP tax will purchase comprehensive health care for themselves and their dependents. Unlike many taxes, the benefits of which are invisible, all will see the additional value they will derive from the tax dollars they will be asked to pay.

Consider, for example, an hourly wage earner working for $9.00 per hour, forty hours per week for an employer that provides no health benefit. This individual, now unable to afford health insurance and unable to pay for anything more than the most basic care, will pay roughly $26.46 per week for full health coverage. If by chance, this individual has non-income-earning dependents, the same $115 per month will also purchase comprehensive care for each and every dependent.

The NHCP Tax is a proportionate tax. The wealthy will pay a larger dollar amount but the same proportionate share of their income. Those paying a large amount of tax will, at least, know that their tax dollars are not only providing something of real and measurable value to their fellow citizens, but also of value to themselves.

The impact on employers will vary according to the level of benefit they are now offering to their employees. Clearly those employers that make no contribution will feel the sting of the additional 5.9 percent of payroll taxes, which will be their responsibility. For the smallest businesses such an increase will pose a modest hardship. Their competitors will have the same obligation, however, so no one will lose a competitive advantage when they pass this cost on to their customers, as all businesses must inevitably do. Considering the benefits the NHCP will bring to the entire nation, it seems like a small price to pay. For many of these businesses the new tax obligation will be comparable to about a six percent across-the-board wage increase and will not put a business in jeopardy. It will, however, provide their employees with an invaluable benefit.

For those employers who offer some level of health benefit to their employees, while contributing their share of the Medicare Tax and paying Workman's Comp premiums, the impact will range from a portion who see their costs increase moderately, to others who will enjoy a savings. All will enjoy the benefit of a workforce free from the burden and distraction of health care bills and just as noteworthy,

99

relief from the process of dealing with health insurers and the annual contract process. Few employers would disagree that this process is an enormous disruption to the daily activities of a successful business.

As with any dedicated tax those who oversee the NHCP from a system-wide perspective will need to assess, each year, the adequacy of the funding. They must do this while balancing the need to conserve tax dollars to the extent possible against the "system imperative" that primary care physicians must be receiving sufficient revenue to insure that their business is successful. This is a non-negotiable element of the NHCP.

We also consider it essential that as many citizens as possible pay their fair share. Part of the logic of the system is that each patient share responsibility for not only their health, but also for the system's financial integrity. Borrowing from the adage that we value the things for which we pay dearly, more than things that are free, we want each taxpayer to value the NHCP as a precious benefit of citizenship.

Potential Savings

Over a ten year period, the first decade of the Twenty-first Century, this National Health Care Plan has the potential to accrue savings to the U.S. Taxpayer measured in the trillions of dollars.

An Associated Press news report in March of 2001 cites an annual report of federal health economists, projecting an increase in health spending from $1.2 trillion in 2001 to $2.67 trillion in 2010. This represents an annual rate of increase of nine percent. The economists further reported that these increases will be driven by the cost of prescription drugs, expected to increase in the same period from 9.4 percent of personal health spending to 16 percent in 2010.

While this author acknowledges that prescription drug costs represent a special challenge, the NHCP is expected to put downward pressure on drug pricing, solely on the basis that the decision-maker, the primary care physician, is also the payer. Today, drugs are prescribed by doctors who have no vested interest in the price of the drugs. When reminded, the doctor might be more inclined to prescribe generic drugs, but often, unless there is a specific request from the patient or the third-party payer, he is too busy. Under the NHCP the rules have changed and the doctor must pay for each prescription he writes. It may not be possible to predict with accuracy how much this will reduce drug prices but it would be naïve to think the doctors decision-making will be unaffected (Mechanic, 1998) or that the pharmaceutical industry will be immune to the pressure of a knowledgeable consumer. In both the Fundholding experiment and the subsequent Primary Care Group program in Great Britain, physicians were responsible for the cost of prescription drugs and it did, indeed, alter their prescribing practices (Bindman, 2001; Jacobs, 1998; Maddox, 1997).

Such an influence is exactly the result we seek by injecting market forces into the process. The drug companies will also face the pressure of market forces, just as will any other producer of goods and services, when they must compete for their customer's business.

A common criticism of health care is that many doctors over-prescribe. Placing financial responsibility for prescription drugs on the physician not only may reduce the cost of drugs, but also improve the quality of care.

We indicated that increases in capitation rates after year two of the NHCP will be tied to the CPI. In Table 7.3, an increase of five percent per year has been arbitrarily selected for illustration purposes as the projected CPI for the first decade of the twenty-first century. Based upon the previous ten years it seems a conservative estimate. When this projection is compared with the federal health economists' projections of an annual increase in health care expenses of nine percent, the potential savings are huge. Should inflation remain low, as in recent years, the savings would be even greater.

To paraphrase the late Senator Everett Dirkson of Illinois, *a hundred billion here and a hundred billion there, and pretty soon your talking real money.*

Experience has shown that programs and controls do not save significant dollars, if any at all. If we are to have any hope at all of reducing health care expenditures the effort must begin with changes in the underlying logic of the system and with the rules of the game. Savings of nearly fifty billion dollars a year would be a phenomenal accomplishment and that is only the beginning under this National Health Care Plan. Accumulated cost-savings, over the next decade, of over three trillion dollars is possible if the American people are willing to push for radical change. Is a plan with the potential to save three trillion dollars over a ten-year period and, improve the quality of care, worth the effort? This is a question only the American people can answer.

The New World of Health Care.

Upon implementation of the National Health Care Plan the world of medicine, whether viewed from the perspective of the patient or the

Table 7.3

COMPARISON OF PROJECTED INCREASES IN HEALTH COSTS
CURRENT HEALTH SYSTEM VERSUS NHCP
2001 - 2010

(In Billions)

	Govt. Projections* @ 9% per yr	NHCP @ 5% per yr	Savings
2001	$ 1,200.0	$ 1,200.0	$ -
2002	1,308.0	1,260.0	48.0
2003	1,425.7	1,323.0	102.7
2004	1,554.0	1,389.2	164.8
2005	1,693.9	1,458.6	235.3
2006	1,846.3	1,531.5	314.8
2007	2,012.5	1,608.1	404.4
2008	2,193.6	1,688.5	505.1
2009	2,391.1	1,772.9	618.2
2010	2,606.3	1,861.6	744.7

Accumulated Savings for the ten year period = $ 3,138.0

*As reported by the Associated Press, 2001

provider, or whether looking at the practice of medicine or the business of medicine, will undergo a transformation. Physicians will control the health care system. Some will argue that physicians will not be effective because of their vested interests, but consider the facts. Our system today simply does not work in spite of the billions of dollars expended to monitor eligibility for care or to place controls on physician utilization patterns and performance.

The fundamental truth is we must place our trust in someone, so who should it be? Government bureaucrats and insurance professionals, regardless of how competent they might otherwise be, lack the knowledge to perform this function well and they are too far removed from the point at which clinical decisions are made. Experience has already demonstrated how ineffective this approach has been. Primary care physicians offer a logical alternative. In general physicians are professionals with a high level of commitment to their patients and they are the individuals who make the decisions in the current system anyway. Stated another way, physicians are the only professionals in a position to exert meaningful control, so why don't we acknowledge that reality and move forward with a system that provides incentives for providing quality care and places controls within the process. Yes, there are concerns that physician decision-making will be unduly influenced by financial pressures but the evidence suggests otherwise. Citing an Alpha Center report from July of 1997, Leiyu Shi and Douglas A. Singh write that *"available evidence suggests that treatment decisions are influenced primarily by clinical factors, not by economic incentives"* (Shi and Singh, 2001).

It will no longer be necessary to have a centralized eligibility-verification process as all Americans will be eligible for coverage. If an individual has a social security number and has made a PCP selection, they are eligible for care. The physician's office needs only to know that the patient they are treating is a member of their patient panel. All government needs to know is that the social security number is valid and is not being used in multiple locations.

In the following chapters we will postulate on the new universe of health care and the practice of medicine under the National Health Care Plan. What will it mean to the American citizen? What will happen to the hundreds of thousands of employees in the health insurance, managed care and other health-related industries, including employees of government agencies, when their services are no longer required? How will this plan change the medical profession? How will it change the way the primary care physician cares for his patients? What about the role of specialists and other medical professions such as chiropractors and podiatrists? How will the NHCP change the world for hospitals, labs and imaging centers, urgent care centers and other ancillary providers? How will it change the work for nurses and other medical professionals and support staff? What about long-term care facilities and also the pharmaceutical industry, both manufacturer and retail?

Medicare and Medicaid pose significant challenges to providers who treat eligible patients. The process itself is cumbersome as a significant amount of paperwork is required and this activity adds cost to the provider's operation. But as frustrating and costly as the process may be, it is in the reimbursement that the real damage is done. Consider just a few examples:

	Provider Charges	Medicare Approved	Medicare Paid
A family physician removes a suspicious Lesion from the body of a Medicare Patient	$80.00	$46.84	$37.47
Vaccination – Influenza & Pneumonia	$40.5	$23.83	$23.83
Tissue Exam by Pathologist	$180	$74.69	$59.75
Hospital Emergency room visit	$228	$93.22	$74.58
Emergency Ambulance Service	$175	$131.11	$104.89
Radiological Interpretation –Chest	$33	$8.98	$7.18

CHAPTER 8

PRIMACY OF PRIMARY CARE

One of the perceived problems in our current health care system, particularly in the last twenty years, has been the diminished interest in primary care on the part of physicians entering the private practice of medicine. The resulting proliferation of subspecialties contributes to the problem of limited access to care and to its rising cost (Grumbach, 1999; Kindig, 1997).

More physicians practicing in ever-narrowing subspecialties also creates pressure for PCPs to defer to their specialty colleagues on a wide range of issues and for a large number of procedures that formerly were the province of the general practitioner. The existence of specialists in a given field begs the question regarding the appropriateness of a PCP's activity therein. The matter comes to a head in cases with problem outcomes and the perception, whether true or not, is that a PCP is less qualified and should have referred the case to a specialist. This activity is seen as an increased liability and will result in higher malpractice premiums for the primary care physician. This has become a powerful force driving PCPs to make more and more specialty referrals while, concomitantly, in managed care the PCP's feel pressure to reduce referrals to specialists and perform procedures that were formerly the province of specialists (Michael, 1998).

We would agree that there are many procedures where the PCP should defer, but there are many others that have traditionally been performed by the PCP, and in which the PCP is more than adequately trained and prepared.

Determining that point where the benefit to the patient is better served by a specialist in lieu of the primary care practitioner and, hence, justifies the additional cost, will always be a matter of judgment. It is our contention that the pendulum has swung too far. What has evolved is a self-perpetuating process where the more specialists there are, the more frequently the PCP will defer, and the more the PCP defers, the greater the demand for specialists.

One can only speculate why so many new physicians choose a specialty practice over primary care. Possibly the promise of more income and more prestige, a less intrusive practice, or even a desire to avoid the need to develop a relationship with one's patients (Grumbach, 1999). It seems safe to assume that most if not all of these issues come into play and undoubtedly there are other influences.

One of the underlying assumptions of this National Health Care Plan is that a continuation on the path of more and more specialization is not in the best interests of the American people. Neither is it in the best interests of the health care system and the practice of medicine. Medicine like so many things has become too impersonal, and how tragic. What is more personal than our health and our bodies.

In the NHCP it will be the primary care physician's judgment that will rule. The PCP's mandate is to do that which best serves the health of the patient while, simultaneously practicing good stewardship of their practice's resources as well as the taxpayer's dollars. It is our expectation that the PCP will take on more responsibility under our proposal and, when it makes sense, that she will reclaim a larger proportion of the procedures that were once her province. She will leave to the specialist those things that can only be handled by the specialist and whatever else she chooses to refer will be those activities in which she lacks interest and/or confidence.

An example might be a board-certified family physician whose residency training included a rotation in dermatology. It would only seem logical that she handle many of the routine skin problems while relying on her subcontractor for more serious cases.

The case manager role of the PCP in our National Health Care Plan will re-establish the primacy of the primary care physician and create a new paradigm. As case manager, the physician is the leader of the health care team and is the center of the business of medicine. Viewed from a new mental model, we would expect primary care to gravitate to the top of the chart of career options for new physicians.

During the initial years of the NHCP it is difficult to grasp the impact on the existing primary care network when more than forty million new patients come shopping for a physician. They will come from neighborhoods and communities not readily served by the local medical cadre and inconvenient for both provider and patient. They are segments of our community that, previously, were judged as clearly unattractive and probably unprofitable by a medical community rapidly gravitating toward the suburbs and upscale urban neighborhoods (Weiss, 1997; Armstrong, 1998). It is a scenario that creates opportunity for new physicians facing a career choice.

The cash flow nature of the NHCP would make it possible for new physicians to move quickly into under-served areas and move just as quickly to a level of profitability. The new PCP will have the cash to make the capital investments necessary to establish an office and hire staff and still begin reducing what, for many, is an imposing indebtedness resulting from their medical education. These men and women will quickly begin to generate the income necessary to begin a life and to make a home for themselves and their families. These will be powerful incentives to help draw the best young physicians to primary care and it will be a while before we need worry about too many.

One would anticipate a reduction in the number of new specialists flowing into the medical community until a new equilibrium has been reached, one in which specialists are common only in those venues requiring training of a highly specialized nature. As the NHCP matures, patterns will emerge to help identify, in each community, the disciplines that are in demand. Recall that the PCP will be the customer/buyer of services in this portion of the health care market.

In the National Health Care Plan it is the primary care physician who is at the center of the care-delivery process. It is the PCP who controls the capitation revenue. It is the PCP who selects subcontracting providers to whom she will refer and into which she will admit. It is the PCP who will decide whether revenue should be used for capital investments in technology to expand her own practice capability. Finally, it is the PCP whose standards of care must be met and ultimately it is the PCP who must satisfy her patients.

A sixty-seven year old man hadn't felt good for weeks. Earlier in the year he had undergone treatment for a serious health problem that ultimately required surgery. The surgery was successful and the patient was released from the specialist's care, except for semi-annual follow-up visits. He was also put on medication that, he was instructed, would be necessary for the long term.

Initially the patient felt great, better than he had for years, but by the time of his first follow-up visit he reported that he had begun to feel poorly. The specialist gave him a thorough examination but found no evidence of a recurrence of his illness. The patient was advised to follow-up with his family doctor.

After a complete physical the family physician could find no apparent cause for the patient's complaints, although the patient insisted that he felt increasingly worse. Consultation with another specialist whom the patient had visited for an earlier illness revealed no evidence that the former ailment had recurred. It was only on a subsequent visit with his family doctor that it was discovered that the patient's new medications could be interacting with another drug the patient had been taking since the first illness. Once a new drug protocol was initiated the patient almost immediately felt better.

CHAPTER 9

PRIMARY CARE UNDER THE NHCP

The Primary Care Physician, regardless of the legal structure in which he works, will function as an independent businessman and will be accountable to his patient/customers. Within reasonable limits and guidelines a patient/customer who is unhappy with the care provided will be free to take his business elsewhere. As we have discussed, this is a component that is delicate but critical to the success of the National Health Care Plan, as freedom to exercise a consumer's right to purchase is a powerful force that will reward physicians who provide high quality care and penalize those who do not.

Primary care physicians who are already affiliated with a group or hospital-based practice will continue as a part of that business organization. The manner in which the practice is structured and the way its physicians are compensated will alter neither the flow of capitation revenue nor the scope of the responsibility the physician bears for his patients. The market is still driven by the perceived attractiveness of a PCP's practice to the consumer/patient who must select a specific primary care physician.

There will be no restrictions on the freedom of physicians to link with other physicians, with hospitals or other business entities. These affiliations and joint ventures are expected to enhance the provider's ability to deliver comprehensive care to their patients in the most cost-effective manner. Physician entrepreneurship is viewed as a good thing. As long as effective incentives are in place we can rely on market forces to determine the most cost-effective way to provide quality health care. We want a system in which physicians must compete for their share of the patient market.

The world in which the primary care physician will practice will be irrevocably changed. No longer will the PCP worry about how he will be paid. No longer will PCPs need to be concerned about the idiosyncrasies of a large number of insurance carriers and managed-care entities. No longer will the financial success of a practice be determined by the density of its appointment calendar or by the effectiveness of its billing and collections system.

The primary care physician will be free to practice the kind of medicine he wants, utilizing the resources for which he is willing to pay, but with this freedom comes responsibility and accountability for the quality of the care he provides. The absence of the insurance and managed care industries does not minimize this accountability. The efforts of these third parties, to control or influence quality have been ineffectual and, more often than not, functioned as an impediment to quality. Physicians will continue, however to be accountable to their peers as well as to their patients and the customer/supplier relationship with the specialist community will elevate the importance of peer review.

The business relationship between the PCP and his specialist subcontractors will require that the primary care physician assess the value and quality of the subcontractor's work. When the PCP is not happy with that quality and is unable to resolve his concerns through interaction and negotiation with the specialist, he will have the option of deleting that specialist from his list of subcontractors. We would anticipate that, as is the case in our current health care system, only in extreme situations would a physician bring a colleague's perceived poor quality to the attention of the medical society or hospital staff committee. A primary care physician will not hesitate, however, to drop a specialist from his subcontractor panel if he loses confidence in that colleague's ability.

Given the close working relationship between the primary care physician and the specialist, the latter will also be in a position to observe the quality of medicine practiced by the PCP. Here again we anticipate little change in the specialist's reluctance to report a primary care colleague's questionable practices unless they are extraordinary. The specialist may be quick, however, to disassociate himself from a customer/colleague, although one would hope that an effort to resolve the concern through discussion and or education would be the first step. In any event, this ability or power to choose with whom one does business can and will have a powerful positive influence on the quality of medical care provided under the NHCP.

The primary care physician's accountability to his patients is paramount to the success of the National Health Care Plan. If a patient is dissatisfied to the point that his concerns cannot be resolved through discussions with his doctor or the physician's staff, the patient is free to leave and when they do so they will take their portion of the PCP's revenue stream with them. "... *patients and physicians must be active drivers of competition. It is not enough for patients [or PCPs] to complain about quality. They must be willing to withdraw their business from low quality providers*" (Dranove, 2000). While the loss of an isolated patient here and there may seem insignificant to the PCP, should patient discontent grow, the resulting exodus could easily deplete a physician's patient panel. The physician's business is in jeopardy whenever revenues are routinely inadequate to cover operating expenses. In this regard a medical practice is no different than any other business.

In light of this issue of the primary care physician's accountability to the patient, the prudent physician will want to place development of patient relationships near the top of his priority list. He will take a little more time to get to know his patients and will find it advantageous to discuss his clinical decisions with the patient. In an ever-increasing percentage of cases the patient may well participate in the decision-making process. One of the keys to the success of the NHCP is a patient's willingness to accept responsibility for his or her own health and effectively become a partner with the physician in the health optimization process (Kindig, 1997). This is one of the critical differences between the NHCP and the current system and we will discuss this further.

Primary Care

An entirely new set of rules governs the primary care game. Similar to the prepaid/full risk HMO environment, the emphasis of the medical practice and a significant portion of the activity will shift away from a focus on reactive medicine and billable services. Packed schedules and strategic billing will contribute nothing to the financial success of the practice and will interfere with the PCP's objectives as case manager. Neither does allegiance to traditional medicine, with focus solely on reactive treatment, foster the long-term best health of the patient population.

The path to the new health care model is through case management. As case manager, the primary care physician will still be responsible for treating illness and injury, but those activities are only components of a larger role. The shift in the PCP's paradigm must happen quickly, but it will not be like clicking a mouse. On the first day of life under the NHCP the transitioning physician's schedule will still be packed and she must find a way to break out of the routines of the past. Patients will also be re-learning the routines. PCPs who attempt to preserve their old ways will find themselves struggling to establish any control over their time and activities. They will be stuck in a reactive mode and will begin to fall behind their colleagues in almost every measure, across all venues. Time and again they will be confronted with illness that could have been prevented and illnesses where the severity could have been mitigated had the case manager been pro-active.

The forward thinking PCP will step back and consider her objectives in this new paradigm. She will begin to reallocate resources so that she can learn as much about her patients as possible for the more intimately familiar she becomes with their lives and their histories, the more she can preserve or restore their health. Physicians will quickly see that their time is still a scarce resource and that it must be devoted to the activities that will produce the best outcomes and that will create value within the context of the new game. Doctors will differ, of course, in the aspects of medical practice from which they derive the most enjoyment and satisfaction. One PCP may want to delegate many of the most routine functions to physician extenders and other well-trained staff so she can focus on serious health problems, while others may choose another focus.

Nothing will change, however, unless the primary care physician takes the time to take inventory of the resources at her command and then reallocates those resources to achieve very specific objectives.

Objective #1 – Know the patient.

A practice may assign staff with both clinical and data-base-management training to develop files on each patient. These files would include, but go beyond the traditional medical history. The question is, what can the patient and physician do, working together, to optimize the patient's health. Through interviews, life-style assessments can be made and risks identified in preparation for development of an "individual health care plan." Such a plan is best created by patient and physician in tandem and both will share responsibility for its development, implementation and periodic review. Issues will include:

1. Treatment for current health conditions whether chronic or acute.
2. A schedule for periodic checkups that delineates the specific examinations, diagnostic tests and immunizations that are planned in response to the unique characteristics of the patient.
3. Medication plan to identify the drugs that are needed and to assure that, when multiple medications are indicated, the best combination of medicine is prescribed. The physician will want to be open with the patient with regard to the cost of drugs and the availability and advisability of generic substitutes.
4. Plans for life-style changes that might include diet, vitamins and supplements, exercise, education, smoking cessation, drug and alcohol treatment, stress reduction and emotional well-being, etc.

Their participation elicits a commitment on the part of the patient to accept responsibility for their own health. As serious health problems occur this sets the stage for a full buy-in of the patient in the specific individual treatment plan. As was the case with medications, the PCP will want to be frank with the patients about the importance of developing the most cost-effective course of action. Optimizing cost-effectiveness serves the best interests of both patient and doctor. The more efficiently routine care and wellness can be provided the more resources will be at hand to respond to exceptional needs that may arise.

Access to a well-designed database on the patient population offers many benefits beyond the planning, care and treatment of individual patients. The ability to search a database, for example, can provide a list of all smoking patients to target for smoking cessation programs. Identifying all pregnant patients would facilitate improved prenatal care through education and other proactive programming. The list of similar benefits is as long as one's imagination.

Objective #2 – Resource allocation

The staffing requirements of even solo practices will change significantly. Because the primary care physician's responsibilities will expand in the National Health Care Plan's case management role, most practices will re-assign and re-train existing staff and some will elect to add staff. Payroll hours devoted to filing insurance claims and patient billing, for example, will disappear and the physician will want to reallocate these resources. The skill sets required may also change.

An effective practice must have that mix of support staff that will permit each physician, whatever his skills and special interests, to make optimum use of his time.

The staff of a practice in this new era must be highly trained and committed to excellence in both care and service for the patients. Resources will be allocated strategically to facilitate staying well-informed about the health issues of each patient in the practice through various levels of contact. Time must be budgeted for the patients with both the most demanding issues as well as for the healthy patient. Staff will want to provide a steady stream of information about health issues pertinent to the characteristics of each family, to elicit their participation in preventive education, and to support them in those efforts.

The typical staffing plan for a practice will strive to provide the following support:

1. Traditional support personnel to:
    - Assist with daily patient encounters within the office
    - Provide the clerical and administrative support for such functions as reception, appointment scheduling, medical records and data-base management

2. Clinical support staff, some of which will be non-traditional:
    - Physician extenders to provide some routine care of patients
    - Staff to conduct personal history interviews and to create and update database files
    - Staff to follow patients: in the hospital, who have been referred to specialists or other subcontracted providers
    - Staff to monitor patients on medication
    - Staff to develop and manage annual checkups and educational and preventive programs

3. Other administrative support staff to:

- Manage accounts payable to subcontractors and Incurred But Not Reported (IBNR) costs
- Provide office management and supervision of staff
- Financial management: accounting, cashflow management, capital planning

4. Some practices will own and operate labs and radiology equipment, necessitating the inclusion of lab and radiological technicians to their staff.

How many staff it will take to perform these functions will vary according to the size (number patients) and complexity (individual or group) of the practice. Whatever the mix it is probable that the ratio of staff with clinical training will increase.

Effective management of payables to specialists, hospitals, and ancillary providers with whom the PCP contracts and effective tracking of IBNR costs is vital as these will be the greatest consumers of cash in the business. Incurred but not reported costs are an estimate of the charges anticipated from subcontractors of all types subsequent to a referral. These future liabilities may be limited to the cost of the office visit or it may be extensive. If, ultimately, a referral and office visit to a specialist leads to surgery or other costly treatment, future liabilities may well expand to include surgical fees, diagnostic charges, hospital charges and the cost of medications. Tracking IBNR allows the practice to effectively manage cash flow and the other financial activities of the business. Failing to manage IBNR effectively leaves the practice vulnerable and restricts the provider's ability to plan for and make the capital investment decisions, which are so important to the long-term success of the practice.

A significant adjustment for most practices will be the shift from managing debt to managing cash flow, and the amount of cash to be managed may be substantial. Unlike most businesses the primary care physician in the NHCP will be paid before many expenses are even incurred. Many human beings find it difficult not to spend surplus dollars and the danger inherent in this temptation cannot be understated. Surplus cash must be effectively managed, if for no other reason, that such a resource has significant earnings capability.

It will not be sufficient that the staff, in whatever configuration, be proficient in only the medical and technical skill requirements. The staff of a successful practice will also be well trained in customer relations and customer service. The patient's perception of the quality of their visit to their PCP will be formed much like a visit to a retail store or restaurant. The recollection of a purchase of a quality product will be diminished if the customer feels they were treated poorly by the sales staff just as the memory of a good meal will be tainted if the waiter or waitress performed unsatisfactorily. The converse, that exemplary service has an ameliorative influence on a customer's dissatisfaction with a product or service, is also transferable to the health delivery environment. Because the patient will rarely possess sufficient knowledge to judge the quality of medicine, the importance of customer service is magnified. Recall that in the NHCP the primary care marketplace is relationship and not transaction driven.

A marvelous example of a staff well trained in all aspects of the business of delivery of both care and service, was observed at an orthodontist's office. The operation was a model of efficiency and effectiveness. This practitioner's staff was highly trained in both technical and human relation skills. The practice also enjoyed a functional data collection system that not only found records but was also a source of meaningful information about individual patients and of valuable data regarding the aggregate patient list.

New patients went through the typical medical history inquiries, but not just by filling out forms they received from the receptionist. A staff member actually interviewed new patients to learn as much about them as was possible. The more familiar both the orthodontist and his staff were with the patients the more personal they could be in their interactions with the patient and family.

The orthodontist would join the interview to introduce himself and to answer questions in the few minutes prior to the examination. The examination process was discussed with the family so there would be few surprises.

At the conclusion of the initial interview and examination the staff would take over with all of the preparation that would ultimately result in selection and application of treatment. The orthodontist stepped in at crucial points in the preparation and treatment process whenever his judgment was required or when only his skill would be appropriate. All other preparation activities and ongoing care were performed with great confidence and professionalism by the staff, under the orthodontists supervision. One of the interesting side

117

benefits of this approach was that in spite of the high volume of patients in the building at any one time, the atmosphere was always calm and professional. If the competence of the staff had not been so apparent, the practice would have appeared casual and nonchalant.

PCP Relationship

David L. Schiedenmayer, MD writes:
"Unfortunately there seems to [be a] variation in a physician's ability to listen to patients" (Quoted in Kilner, 1998).

This is a common observation of patients who add that there is also a variance in the physician's <u>willingness</u> to listen. There may exist a small percentage of physicians who consider it unnecessary to listen but for most it is simply a matter of priorities. Time is scarce and many physicians feel pressured to move quickly from one patient encounter to the next, particularly when a physician is delayed in reaching his office. Like other human beings, physicians may assume they know what the patient will say and may even listen but not hear. Because of their intelligence and extreme confidence, physicians may be more prone to these lapses than others

The National Health Care Plan will encourage and foster intimate communication between the patient and physician. The physician will still be busy, but priorities have shifted along with his mental model. The patient is now a customer whose satisfaction is essential to the continuing flow of revenue. No longer will the PCP find it necessary to balance between FFS and managed care. The doctor will be accountable only to the patient, a patient who comes to him by choice and who has the freedom to take his stream of capitation revenue down the street.

Also important is that communication between the physician and his patients, and between the physician's staff and the patient, signals a different role and status for the patient. No longer just an encounter, patients will be a party to the health delivery process and will have clear responsibilities that serve both their own interests and those of the provider. As we noted above the patient must share in the responsibility for their health and care. Knowledge is power and ignorance diminishes power. The prudent PCP will be open about both the medical and financial variables involved in selecting the best course of action.

While true that there is a point at which the patient's comprehension of the medical science will begin to diminish, the American patient can understand a great deal more than we give credit. The more patients understand, the more they will play their part rather than be the passive recipient of care. The more patients understand the more tolerant they will be of disappointing outcomes. It is, in fact, amazing how reasonable people can be when treated reasonably. As we have noted, patients who understand that medicine is an uncertain science, and as much a craft as a science, will understand that physicians are fallible human beings doing their best. Those who view their physicians as a god expect perfection and when the outcome is disappointing they are more likely to conclude that someone erred and, to seek redress.

Finally, it has long been proven that human beings invest more of themselves when they have ownership. The objective of the physician must be to foster this sense of proprietorship. Not all patients will respond. There will always be individuals who cling to ignorance and apathy. Over time, we believe, the American people will begin to learn how vital it is that they participate and take responsibility. In doing so they gain a fuller understanding of the case management role of their PCP and they also gain better health.

Case Management

The crucial role of case management in the National Health Care Plan merits further discussion. At first glance the reader is likely to conclude that by case management we are referring to the "gatekeeping" concept central to the HMO environment. There certainly are parallels between case management in the NHCP and the gatekeeper role in the HMO, but there are also significant differences. Unfortunately, gatekeeping has taken on a pejorative connotation, as it has been cited as one of the most unpopular aspects of the HMO experience. We ask the reader to tread carefully here and not make assumptions or draw premature conclusions leading to a rejection of case management.

In the National Health Care Plan case management refers to the role of the primary care physician. The PCP's responsibilities transcend that which we have learned to expect from the family doctor or general practitioner in the current health care system and these responsibilities are not limited to treating injury and illness in a reactive mode. The PCP must do more than wait for the patient complaint. He is responsible for both preserving and restoring the health of his patients and he is entrusted with a portfolio of resources that are fully at his command. The physician can use these resources as imaginatively as he wishes, not only to provide care within his area of practice and competency, but also to purchase care beyond that which he himself can provide.

The case management role does not end when the PCP makes a referral and purchases care from other providers. When making a referral the PCP is delegating responsibility to a colleague with special expertise. He is neither transferring nor abdicating responsibility for the patient's care. Whatever the outcome of the subcontractor's contribution it is the PCP whom the patient will hold accountable. However complicated the patient's health problem may be and however many specialty, institutional and ancillary providers may be asked to contribute, it is the primary care physician's responsibility to see that every protocol, every procedure and every medication is a component of a coordinated plan of action. The PCP must also keep the patient informed and up-to-date, a responsibility at which few providers excel in the existing health care system.

Unlike the gatekeeper in the managed care venue, it is the PCP who selects the providers from the medical community. Whereas the gatekeeper functions as a referral coordinator pursuant to the rules of the managed care organization and consistent with the list of covered benefits, the case manager establishes his own rules governing the referral process and selects any course of treatment that he deems appropriate.

The gatekeeper strives to control utilization to meet the financial objectives of an organization far removed from the patient and with which he often has only a contractual agreement. He also functions in a fiscal environment that is almost always poorly funded. The case manager in the NHCP is working to balance the needs of his patient, whom he must look in the eye and with whom he must share his own financial and practice objectives. The environment in which the case manager functions will be adequately funded. The result is that all medically accepted treatment protocols appear on his menu.

Unlike the gatekeeper who:

- Has limited latitude for creative solutions and who is constrained by a carefully delineated list of covered services, and
- Is required to get prior approval to employ many of these services,

the case manager has no such constraints. The PCP has extraordinary latitude to utilize any and all available tactics to meet the needs of the patient. Other than not deviating too far beyond the boundaries of accepted medical standards, the only approval the PCP must obtain is that of the patient, the patient's family and his own professional conscience. He may also consult with appropriate specialty providers to solicit their input prior to making a decision and although he is well-advised to do so, the ultimate decision is his and his alone. This is far removed from an environment where a treatment plan and other medical decisions are scrutinized by a panel of professionals with little or no relationship with the patient.

Case management is both central and essential to the success of the NHCP. The objective of case management is to enable the PCP to serve the interests of his patients while effectively and efficiently employing the scarce resources at his disposal. The objective of gatekeeping, on the other hand, is to control utilization and cost without increasing the risk to the patient. The differences are like night and day.

Capitation Revenue

In exchange for her commitment to optimize the health of her patient population the primary care physician will receive revenue on a per patient basis. As noted, the capitation revenue is received at the beginning of every month and this will be the sole source of revenue. It has also been noted that one of the objectives of the NHCP is to insure that the capitation rates are adequate for the physician to meet the needs of her patients and to provide a healthy return on her investments. At any point in the process, if it were to become impossible to maintain profitability, no matter how diligent the physician, the system will begin to fail.

As has been repeated to the edge of redundancy, the adequacy of capitation revenue is paramount to the success of this National Health

Mel Hawkins

Care Plan. But how much is enough? Are the gross health care dollars expended in the U.S. adequate to insure that primary care physicians can deliver quality care to their sick patients and still be financially successful? This proposal is grounded in the belief that such funds are, indeed, adequate.

Table 9.1

PROJECTED CAPITATION PAYMENTS TO PCPs UNDER
THE NHCP
Data Using 1999 Census

Total Health Expenditures for Health Services and Supplies*	1133.1 Billion
Less: 5 Percent for first year "Catch-up Care"	56.7 Billion
Net Revenue available for Cap Distribution	1,076.4 Billion
Estimated U.S. Population for 1999**	272,691,000
Annual Expenditures per capita	$ 3,947
Monthly Expenditures per capita	$ 329

*U.S. Census, Statistical Abstracts of the United States, Table No. 160
**U.S. Census, Statistical Abstracts of the United States, Table No. 2

So, how much revenue can the PCP expect to receive?

Absent the actuarial work, capitation rates can only be estimated in the widest of swaths, but the result will, nevertheless, be instructive. This estimate is the result of an analysis considering a number of assumptions using data from Table 9.1.

Physician practices will vary when compared by any number of criteria. For our purposes we are assuming that the prototypical physician practice is an exact cross-section of the population. Although there will be a wide variance in the number of patients a primary care physician can handle, for the purpose of this illustration we assume a PCP, in solo practice, may be willing and able to handle a total caseload of between 1000 and 2000 patients. Based upon our assumptions we can estimate the capitation revenue that will flow to the PCP in year one as illustrated in Table 9.2.

Table 9.2

CAPITATION REVENUE PER PCP, PER MONTH/PER YEAR
By Patient Caseload

Year 1

Caseload of 1000 patients	$ 329,000 per mo. $ 3,948,000 per yr.
Caseload of 1500 patients	$ 493,500 per mo. $ 5,922,000 per yr
Caseload of 2000 patients	$ 658,000 per mo. $ 7,896,000 per yr.

Year 2

Caseload of 1000 patients	$ 346,000 per mo. $ 4,152,000 per yr.
Caseload of 1500 patients	$ 519,000 per mo. $ 6,228,000 per yr
Caseload of 2000 patients	$ 692,000 per mo. $ 8,304,000 per yr.

Once the annual capitation revenue to be received by each physician has been estimated, one can only make a judgment about the adequacy of these dollars relative to the PCP's ability to provide comprehensive care for his patients. In making this judgment, recall that a portion of this cash will be spent on reinsurance to protect the physician from catastrophic claims. Consider as well that during the first year a fund has been established to help cover the cost of care for those whose medical needs went unattended under the previous system and that these dollars, in year two, will be added to the distributed capitation revenue.

The fiscal impact on each community can also be estimated although there may be some variation from one area of the country to another. As an example the total cap revenue flowing into a metropolitan area of 300,000 would be over one-and-a- quarter billion dollars every year. For some communities this may result in a net increase in local health care expenditures and for others it may reduce total health care revenue exchanged in the local economy.

Hundreds of thousands of dollars flowing to primary care physicians, at the beginning of each month will bring about stunning changes in practice financial management. At once, primary care medicine becomes a cash flow business. It is the subject of every financial manager's dreams. Cash revenue in hand, from sales, before suppliers must be paid.

Costs and Incentives in Case Management.

Physicians, hospitals and other providers will no longer be fighting with insurance companies, HMOs and other managed care organizations. They will now be partners under the leadership of the PCP case manager in the sense that they have only one mission: to keep patients healthy and happy. This will be accomplished by providing cost-effective care of the highest quality.

Financial success will be a function of patient satisfaction. Primary care physicians must satisfy their customers (patients) in order to win the customer's loyalty and retain their business. Specialists, hospitals and other providers must also satisfy the patient but it is the satisfaction of the primary care physician that will protect market share and enable growth. The primary care physician is the subcontractor's customer in all respects and a PCP's satisfaction is earned through the provision of exemplary care to the PCP's patients. As was noted earlier, the relationships are equivalent to the supply chain in the world of original equipment manufacturers.

What do we see in business and industry? Companies striving continuously to improve the quality, cost, and the appeal of their products and services or they go out of business. Customers and suppliers become informal partners in a venture in which the futures of both are at risk. In recent years, facilitated by Massachusetts Institute of Technology and other of the nation's top universities, supply chain management has become a recognized discipline of study of how customers and suppliers can work together for their mutual benefit. For the customer, the OEM, it is essential that they have an optimal supply chain, one where they receive the best combination of quality and pricing, thus assuring their ability to compete in their market. The supplier's interests are parallel in that their reward for contributing to their customer's optimal supply chain is the commitment from that customer of a steady stream of business and for the opportunity to grow their business as their customer's business grows.

A similar commitment on the part of primary care physicians and their subcontractors, whether professional, institutional or ancillary providers, will prove to be pivotal to their success under the National Health Care Plan.

Successful providers, like successful businesses everywhere, are those that distinguish themselves from the competition.

When we laid out the ground rules for this analysis we warned that there is no such thing as a perfect human system and certainly not a perfect health care system. Since we cannot achieve perfection we must have a system that is driven to quality. Another lesson from industry is that "one cannot inspect quality into a product." Quality must be designed into the production process. Quality is built into the system because it is only through quality – defined as customer satisfaction – that incentives come. The incentive, as in any other free market enterprise, is profit.

This lesson is documented throughout the experience of our capitalist economy. With the exception of such products as utilities, which are supplied by an oligopoly, it is virtually impossible to control production of goods and services through regulation. We rely on free market forces to insure quality and it works.

The state of the current health care system in the United States should be sufficient evidence that regulation and external controls provide a poor substitute for the economic incentive that is a return on capital.

Reinsurance

One of the challenges to a capitated, full-risk program is that there are a small proportion of patients who suffer "catastrophic" illnesses and injuries. These cases are a catastrophe for the at-risk physicians as well, because a single case can eat up significant chunks of the physician's available cash and threaten one of the critical elements of the NHCP, the assurance that physicians can be profitable. Reinsurance provides such assurance, that even those patients with high-cost health problems will receive adequate care and will not be passed around by providers trying to avoid the financial responsibility.

The question is not whether reinsurance should be purchased, but rather, who should do the purchasing and how much should they purchase? The easiest solution would be to ask government to provide this coverage, but this runs counter to our objective which is to minimize the role of government. Instead it is proposed that every dollar that can be distributed to primary care physicians through capitation payments, be distributed. Reinsurance is a product that can be provided by the free market and the NHCP envisions that the PCPs will, at their discretion, purchase whatever level of coverage they require to feel secure. It is difficult to imagine that a PCP would be so short sighted as to eschew reinsurance and sacrifice their long-term security for short-term savings. Those few that elect such a path will suffer the natural consequences. These natural consequences are far more effective than any efforts we might make to regulate such behavior.

The re-insurance industry is one in which quality and competitiveness will be driven by market forces and there seems no reason to involve government beyond the traditional role of state insurance commissions.

The cost of the "catch up" care can also be handled through the reinsurance coverage purchased by the PCP. The following example is offered but the reader is cautioned that the numbers are for illustration only and may not represent the levels of coverage purchased by a primary care physician or the terms of the coverage.

To keep the example as simple as possible, assume the PCP purchases reinsurance to protect himself from extraordinary costs above $20,000 per patient. The PCP will be responsible for 100 percent of the first $20,000, at which point the reinsurance kicks in per a 20/80 arrangement. From that point forward the PCP pays 20 percent of any costs and the reinsurer pays 80 percent. Assume also that the PCP share of this excess cost is limited to another $20,000.

Table 9.3

REINSURANCE COPAYMENT SCHEDULE
Based on 20/80 split
and $20,000 Deductible

	PCP	Reinsurance
First $20,000	$ 20,000	$ -
Next $100,000	$ 20,000	$ 80,000
Over $120,000	0%	100%

One scenario for the "catch up" care might be that the Federal Government will share the cost of care for eligible patients with both the PCP and the Reinsurance company on a fifty/fifty basis during the first year of the plan, with the amount to be paid out of the NHCP Fund. At the end of the first year of the National Health Care Plan the catch-up provision will expire and the PCP and his re-insurer will become fully responsible.

Table 9.4

REINSURANCE COPAYMENT SCHEDULE WITH CATCH-UP CARE ELIGIBILITY
Federal Subsidy of Fifty Percent of Cost
for Both PCP and Reinsurance Company

	PCP	Reinsurance	U.S. Govt
First $20,000	$ 10,000	$ -	$ 10,000
Next $100,000	$ 10,000	$ 40,000	$ 50,000
Over $120,000	$ -	50%	50%

Specialists, Hospitals and Other Providers

For the primary care physician in his function of case manager, the services of every provider of a health service or product in the community will be a resource at his disposal as he searches for optimal solutions to medical problems and health issues. These services – whether specialty medical practices, hospitals, laboratories, imaging centers, urgent care centers, out-patient surgical centers, physical therapy clinics, long term care facilities, home health care agencies, hospice programs, medical equipment and prosthetic suppliers, pharmacies, or others – exist in the National Health Care Plan to serve the case manager in his efforts to administer to the needs of his patients. As such each provider will be challenged to justify their existence by meeting the needs of their customer/PCP.

Whether all of these providers are necessary will be determined by the perceived value of their product or service in the mind of the customer/PCP in his quest for optimal care for his patients. These subcontracting providers will be competing for a finite amount of health care revenue. There will be no free rides and some providers will not survive because their product or service is not competitive and others will fail because their product or service is not valued. The only thing that counts is the subcontractor's ability to provide value. New providers will emerge who offer new and innovative solutions to their customers.

When value is demonstrated the PCP will be quick to add that provider to his care team and the expectation will be that the subcontractor accept the role of team member. The primary care physician will work to develop close relationships with his subcontractors as such relationships will be a key to success.

Mel Hawkins

The largest nursing home in its state had evolved from a county poor house, to a tuberculosis hospital and then to a 500-bed nursing home. The facility operated out of a large complex, half of which was relatively new construction, less than twenty years old, and the other half was comprised of sections that ranged from fifty to one hundred years of age.

One's expectation upon learning of the facility's history, and prior to a visit, would be to find an old, highly institutional operation that did little more than provide custodial care to its resident population. What first time visitors found instead was a remarkably caring and professional atmosphere, with a staff that took great pride in the quality of care they provided. The largest portion of the facility was devoted to intermediate nursing care and the remaining portions housed a skilled care unit, an Alzheimer's unit, a ward for individuals severely impaired as the result of closed-head injuries, and a residential care unit.

The facility had also received national recognition for its prevention, care and treatment of pressure sores, to the extent that it was considered a teaching facility and test ground for products used for the care of this common problem. The facility was also recognized nationally for its dietary programs.

As one might imagine, the facility's population had a high proportion of residents on Medicaid. Given the size and age of the facility it was costly to run. Because of the criteria by which requests for increases in Medicaid funding were reviewed and adjudicated, each year the Medicaid rates increased at a declining rate. It was a complicated formula, but the crux of it was that rate increases were set in relation to a baseline cost for the facility from a given point in time. Each year increases in Medicaid payments fell further and further behind actual costs until the facility found itself in financial trouble.

The only way to get a significant increase, in order to keep abreast of the cost of doing business, was for an LTC entity to undergo a change of ownership. Private, for-profit LTC companies responded by selling off a facility to other organizations about every five years. A new owner could then apply for Medicaid reimbursement rates based on a newly established baseline.

The financial health of the facility in this example had gradually declined, as it had not been considered possible for it to undergo such an ownership transition. Eventually a way was discovered, but by this time the quality of the programs and staff had eroded significantly. The ownership was transitioned to a not-for-profit group established for this specific purpose. Although the rates were re-adjusted, the damage had been done and the new management was faced with an almost insurmountable challenge as it worked to return this facility to its former glory and status as an exemplary provider.

Medicaid rules and regulations prevailed, in this and other examples, but the big losers were the residents of these facilities and their families. It is a phenomenon intrinsic to bureaucracies, that the rules of the game become a mission unto themselves, quite apart from the industry's mission to provide quality long-term care to the American people.

CHAPTER 10

LIFE UNDER THE NATIONAL HEALTH CARE PLAN

In this chapter we will examine the other players in the sport of medicine and we will strive to anticipate how their world will change under the National Health Care Plan.

The Patient

The patient must be the focal point of any effective system for delivering health care, for it is the patient whom the provider exists to serve, just as in any commercial market place it is the customer that all serve. Somehow in our existing health care system the patient as customer has slipped out of the sights of many providers. The most obvious and most important impact of the National Health Care Plan with regard to patients, is that they become the focal point of a system in which they are immediately eligible for comprehensive health care purchased totally out of the tax dollars – dollars which they have paid individually and collectively. Not a single American citizen or tax-paying legal alien, need ever worry about the availability of care for themselves and their families. They need never be concerned that a loss or change of jobs could deprive them of coverage. They need never worry that their financial health could be jeopardized by their physical health. We have already noted that medical costs are one of the most common causes of personal bankruptcies in the United States. Under the NHCP we could expect to see these virtually disappear.

These reasons alone would seem to validate the need for the NHCP. Clearly there is no way the existing health system, or any contemplated reform or version thereof, can make such a promise and keep it. The point of this book is that such promises are not now and have never been the objective of the American health care system and the only way they can become our objective is through a redesign and reconstruction of the system itself.

Universal access to comprehensive care is at the top of the list of benefits offered by the National Health Care Plan, but represents only the beginning of the list. One of the most publicized problems of today is the cost of prescription drugs. Under the NHCP all citizens will receive their prescription drugs as a primary benefit. Even if we were speaking only of senior citizens, free prescription drugs would significantly reduce the pain, suffering and worry of the population, not to mention their financial duress. Providing medicines for all citizens will provide benefits beyond measure.

Freedom to choose physicians or change physicians is a wonderful gift. Any one of us could find ourselves in a situation in which we need to find a new doctor and although there will be communities that are under-served, for most people and in most communities there will be doctors actively seeking new patients. Those communities with a shortage of physicians can be identified and that information can be made available to the family practice and other residency programs graduating primary care physicians. Unlike our current system, where these locales are considered undesirable because of their demographics, all communities whether rich or poor, urban, suburban, or rural, white or minority will offer the same cashflow potential. A new primary care physician can move into any community where there are few practicing physicians and begin their practice with a full panel of patients and the revenue that follows with the patients.

The patient will also enjoy a life with full health coverage but no out-of-pocket costs, no forms to file, and only one point of communication. In the event of serious illness or injury there will be no barriers to hospital admission and no hassle at the time of admission.

For parents the comfort of knowing that health care is available to meet the needs of their children is priceless. Imagine a scenario in which a parent has someone to whom they can turn for advice, information, and education about the health of their children; that someone being a physician who is not only available, but has a vested interest in preserving the health of that child. Imagine also a school environment in which every student file includes the name of a primary care physician, the child's medical identification number and, possibly, an executed consent form authorizing the child's physician to provide treatment in the event the parent cannot be reached. The potential benefits of parents, schools and providers working in cooperation for the health of our children are many.

Of great significance is the relationship between the patient and physician. On the surface it may appear that little has changed – the doctor is still the caregiver and the patient is the recipient of care – but nothing is the same. At the core of the relationship is the new reality that the patient has chosen this doctor and is free to alter that choice. The successful physician will be one who understands that he must do more than treat a patient's ailment, he must also satisfy a customer. The difference is subtle but has enormous consequences, similar to the difference between a patient seen by a doctor on duty in an emergency room and one seen in his private practice. In the ER the objective is to address the patient's needs quickly and then move on to the next patient, with no expectation that the doctor will see a patient again. In the ER doctors will invest very little energy in their relationship with the patient. In private practice under the current health care system the relationship becomes important. In the world of the NHCP the physician/patient relationship is paramount.

In the case management venue the relationship takes on a new meaning. The patient now has power and with power comes responsibility. The patient can walk when dissatisfied, but does this really serve that patient's best interests? What the liberated patient wants is a relationship with a professional on whom one can count. The patient wants quality care, of course, but the bottom line is good health and for this the patient must also share responsibility. The physician's best interests are also served by the patient's good health. The doctor cannot guarantee health, he can only improve the odds of good health and he cannot do this alone. The physician needs the full participation of the patient and the patient requires the best efforts of the physician. The physician must know the physical and emotional needs of the patient and the patient must know and understand the physician's needs.

Recall that our objective was to create a scenario in which the interests of the physician and the patient are parallel. The needs of patients are apparent, but what must the patient know about the doctor's interests? The patient must understand that the physician's success, and therefor his ability to serve the patient's interests, depends on his ability to optimize the use of his resources. The interests of neither party are served if, to pacify an unreasonably demanding patient, the doctor orders unneeded tests, medications or treatments.

What is necessary is a level of communication and acceptance of responsibility that is two-way. The patient has a responsibility to ask questions and the doctor has a responsibility to give answers. The objective of the communication is to reach a level of mutual understanding of one another's interests. The patient has the right to request specific treatments, specialists or facilities but he does not have the right to demand these things. Recall that the primary care physician's specialty and hospital preferences should have been among the criteria utilized in the patient's choice of doctors. In any event, the physician, as the professional responsible for the quality of care, must have the final word.

The ideal scenario is one in which the patient understands and both parties agree to:
-A course of treatment and anticipated outcome
-The risks to the patient
-Whether or not a second opinion will be sought
-The cost of the care
-Alternate treatments that were not chosen and why.
-The physician's expectations of the patient
-Next steps

The more the patient understands the alternatives available to them and the associated risks and costs, the more likely all parties will accept the outcome, whether good or bad. The physician must have confidence that their patients are being honest and forthcoming and he also has the right to expect full compliance with directions and instructions. The physician is not without recourse if the patient were to show blatant disregard for medical advice.

Little need be said about the issue of patient privacy. This is a subject of much concern today but one that will be almost totally resolved under the National Health Care Plan. Privacy issues arise as a result of the breadth and scope of the distribution patterns of medical information. Under the NHCP the only entities with access to a patient's medical records will be the primary care physician and the caregivers with whom he contracts. There are no insurance or managed care companies, no Health Care Finance Administration and no workers compensation program to collect and then disseminate information about a patient. There also will be no collections efforts pursuing payment from patients.

The federal government, through the registration process, will manage a database of information about all citizens and legal aliens registered for the plan, but the medical information collected for this database will be limited to such information as blood type, allergies, or organ donor information; none of which are compromising. Special health conditions may also be stored for the benefit of patients whose health would be jeopardized if a provider unfamiliar with a patient's history were to become involved.

In an environment where health care is an entitlement how does one deal with incorrigible patients or physicians. There must be a mediation or arbitration process, short of litigation, to seek resolution of disputes between parties:

- Physicians found to be negligent or abusive can suffer temporary or permanent loss of revenue or they may be required to maintain financial responsibility for the care of patients who have been permitted to seek a new provider. The ultimate penalty is loss of license. Patients must also have access to the courts, although we would anticipate that the volume of litigation would decline under the NHCP.
- Patients found to be abusive or negligent may also be sanctioned, including loss of the right to all or part of their health coverage or they may be required to seek a new physician subject to conditions to which they must consent.

The Specialists

For specialists there will be two changes in the way they go about the business of a medical practice that will be significant. The first relates to the autonomy previously enjoyed by the specialists. In his or her area of expertise the specialist answers to virtually no one in the current health care system. Once a patient is referred to the specialist the role of the family doctor or personal physician is suspended for all practical purposes until the patient is released from the care of that specialist. The family physician receives reports, of course, and may visit a patient who has been hospitalized but typically is not actively involved with the case.

With the exceptions of those specialists who are employed by or contracting with an HMO, the insurance or managed care entity has little influence over the course of treatment selected by a specialist, other than seeking a second opinion. The only other external influence has to do with the payment process through the insurance and managed care company. Unless highly unusual, the procedure proposed by the specialist will almost certainly be approved for coverage, but the specialist may need to obtain pre-certification from the insurer. The insurer or managed care entity will also have an established fee that they are willing to pay for a particular procedural code.

Both of these influences will disappear under the NHCP as the specialist will be acting as a sub-contractor for a primary care physician who will want to be involved in the decision process and the ongoing care and, who will pay the specialist per an agreement negotiated between them. The participation of the PCP will take some getting used to, but it will be part of a relationship between professionals who have a common interest and share a common respect for one another. None of the seemingly arbitrary and impersonal interaction with an insurer will be necessary. Getting paid will be easier and faster as the payer will be involved from the beginning and will derive no benefit from a complicated billing process. The specialist will implement, with the PCP's participation, the treatment plan and will bill the PCP for the agreed upon charge.

In our current system another physician is the referral source of the majority of a specialist's patients although some are self-referred. Under the NHCP all patients under the care of a specialist will come through a primary care physician who serves as case manager. The success, therefore, of a specialty practice will depend on the specialist's ability to develop, nurture and maintain a good working relationship with all of the PCP's from whom she hopes to get referrals. As noted earlier, the specialists will need to compete for a finite book of business and the winners will be those physicians who have earned the greatest amount of professional respect for their expertise, who have demonstrated an ability to work as a member of a PCP's care team, and who charges the most competitive fees.

Hospitals

As we noted in Chapter 2, our nation's hospitals have faced, perhaps, the greatest challenge of all health care providers over the last several decades and the National Health Care Plan will introduce an entirely new set of rules.

Imagine a business environment where there is a steadily declining demand for your product or service, while capital and labor costs escalate and in which the number of regulatory hoops through which one must jump increases exponentially. If you can visualize such an environment then you can begin to comprehend the challenges that American hospitals have faced over the last several decades. Think about the systems and societal changes that have occurred:

- Suburbanization and other population shifts
- Inflation, often double digit
- Recessions
- Technological explosion in health care
- Diagnostic Related Groups (DRGs) and other payment control mechanisms
- Regulation
- Explosive nursing and ancillary wages and salaries
- Surplus beds and dramatically reduced lengths of stay
- Admission pre-certifications
- Urgent and convenient care centers
- Ambulatory surgical centers
- Free-standing and physician-based labs, imaging, physical therapy clinics
- Ever increasing complexity of insurance and managed care claims processing
- Medicare and Medicaid billing
- Enormous increases in capital costs

The National Health Care Plan changes both the rules of the game and the venue in which the game is played. Consider, in broad strokes, how a hospital does business today.

Hospitals are typically paid under some type of cost-based reimbursement format that functions similarly to the fee-for-service world of the physician. To be paid they must submit a bill or claim, usually to a third-party payer pursuant to the unique rules and requirements of that payer. In the case of all admissions where the patient shares the financial responsibility for the hospital's charges, a bill will also be sent to the patient. The hospital's success is contingent upon its ability to:

- Maximize occupancy
- Increase the number of billable services delivered
- Increase the average unit cost of such billable services
- Improve collections performance

In the current system the first and foremost strategy utilized by hospitals is to secure the allegiance of as many physicians as possible. Outside of emergencies, hospital admissions and other utilization of the hospital's services and resources almost universally result from a physician order. Without physicians on staff there would be no non-emergency admissions. The hospital must provide a facility that is not only convenient for the physician but also offers the best possible support. This may mean technology that connects the physician's record system to the hospital as well as technology that is available for the diagnosis and treatment of illness and injury. As with any producer of goods and services the more the hospital can do to make the physician's job easier the more likely will admissions follow. This places a premium on the breadth, scope and quality of technology that may include basic laboratory and radiological capability, CAT Scan and MRI capability. Also important are dialysis capability, state-of-the-art surgical and intensive care capability and the list grows incrementally with each new medical advancement.

These significant capital investments not only secure admissions from local and regional physicians, but they also offer significant billing opportunities. The beauty is that the physician's decision to utilize such technology is not influenced by the cost of the service. The physician may be constrained by the criteria of insurers, both public and private, but cost is rarely of consequence to the physician's business. The insurer or managed care entity will cover almost all of the available diagnostic procedures if the physician determines that the procedure is medically necessary.

The hospital's strategy then is to offer quality care and state of the art technology on both the medical and business sides of the business. The better job the facility does, the more physicians will elect to associate with it. Once the hospital has made a capital investment in new medical technology the key is to encourage its utilization.

Duplication of expensive technology happens as the result of lack of competition and the absence of a knowledgeable customer weighing the value and cost of one service against that of another.

Under the National Health Care Plan the relationship between the hospital, the admitting physicians and the patient changes. A facility's success is still contingent on the hospital's ability to earn the loyalty of the community's physicians, not only because the physician admits, but also because he now pays the bill. The facility now has a knowledgeable customer and one whose own best interests are served by getting the best value for the dollar.

Hospitals will see changes that parallel those experienced by the specialists. There will be no complicated precertification or qualifying procedures, nor will there be rigid length-of-stay guidelines. All admission and discharge decisions will be made locally by physicians with whom the hospital has cultivated a relationship. Incurred charges will be ordered by the physician team and billing will be a simple matter of a posting to the PCP's account, according to whatever terms have been negotiated. Like the specialists, the hospital's book of business will be a function of their ability to satisfy their customer, the PCP, and his patients.

Care provided by the hospital's emergency department will also be easier as, other than patients who are visiting from out of town, the facility will know who to contact and will have general instructions on file from each provider.

Justification for capital investments, whether new medical or business technology, will be determined by real and not artificial demand. As the payor, physicians will order utilization of medical technology only when they believe it will benefit the patient and not solely because it is available with the bill to be paid by a third party. Hospitals, then, will make investments in technology only when the investment can improve the value and quality of the product and/or when it will reduce production costs , much as is true in business and industry everywhere.

In the hospital's business office things will be remarkably different. Although the hospital will still need the information technology to track patient services rendered, the billing process will be relatively simple. The hospital will set up a customer file and will invoice each primary care physician directly. The modern facility will seek to link directly with the PCP's bank to offer direct debits, thus reducing costs on both sides of the billing equation.

The admission process will also be simplified, as no financial or insurance screening will be required. It will be necessary only to swipe the patient's identification card, at which time all the information necessary for billing the primary care physician will be available. Even patients visiting from out-of-town will be simple to admit, as the contact information will be readily available.

It is difficult to estimate the savings to be gained on the business side but it should be substantial, freeing resources to focus on clinical issues where true value to the customer can be created. Recall the reference to the study by PricewaterhouseCoopers that found that, at minimum, one half hour of paperwork is necessary for each hour of patient care under the current system. This will be reduced to virtually nothing beyond capturing of basic clinical information and internal costing data.

Hospitals will find that, as a result of having a knowledgeable, willing and able customer, the competition for business with other hospitals, freestanding ancillary providers and physician-owned alternatives may become fierce. Today it is easy for surpluses to exist in many of these service areas but this will not be the case under the NHCP. Victory will go to those who can provide exemplary service and support at a competitive price. This will likely result in a total reassessment of the strategic positioning of facilities in the community.

Ancillary Providers

For labs, imaging centers, out-patient surgical centers, urgent care centers, physical therapy clinics, home health care agencies, hospice and other providers the business will be handled in a manner virtually the same as for hospitals and specialists. Business will be driven by the relationship these entities can build with the physicians from whom they get referrals. The primary care providers in their geographic marketplace will be the major referral source, although in the case of some ancillary providers, outpatient surgical centers being one example, the specialist may be the referring agent. In any event all decision making will be local.

To what extent will these providers be utilized under the National Health Care Plan? That will depend totally on their ability to serve a need of their customer. If the primary care physician perceives no value in the service, no patients will be referred. If value is perceived the facility will likely be competing for the business with other providers. Where group practices exist, many may elect to provide some of this care within their own facilities and utilizing their own resources.

Labs and imaging centers, particularly those that require significant capital investments, will work hard to develop and maintain relationships with the physicians in their community, particularly the primary care physician. Urgent care centers may also serve a real purpose, as after hours emergency or urgent care is an area where it is difficult for the PCP to control costs. More groups or associations may elect to provide an after hours clinic to keep the business and the revenue that flows from it, in house.

All of the subcontracting providers that offer a valued product or service can expect to see a measurable reduction in the cost of doing business, freeing revenue and resources to improve quality, innovation and training.

Long Term Care

Few components of the health care system are as costly, as complicated, as highly regulated and as suspect as long-term care. Roughly one percent of the population resides in some form of long-term care facility, whether skilled or intermediate care. The industry is characterized by fierce competition both internal and external.

Internally there are for-profit facilities, for-profit chains, not-for-profit and public facilities. These facilities may provide both short- or long-term care, and both skilled and intermediate care. Many also offer custodial care. In recent years we have witnessed the emergence of assisted living facilities that offer an independent living environment offering a range of support services and a very basic level of nursing care.

As the internal competition has heightened, facilities have responded by offering special units for Alzheimer's disease, acquired neurological disorders, infectious diseases, mental disorders, hospice care, day care and respite care.

Externally long-term care facilities must compete with hospitals that, anxious to get a piece of this action, have converted excess acute-care capacity to meet some of these needs. Some focus on transitional and hospice care and some provide skilled or intermediate care.

Home health care agencies also compete for patients by offering nursing support to patients in their own homes as a less-expensive alternative to nursing homes.

In order to maintain an acceptable rate of occupancy long-term care organizations are compelled to market themselves aggressively and most have sizeable advertising and marketing budgets. These facilities also spend considerable sums on interior decorating, furnishings and other amenities as the families of prospective residents, particularly the affluent, unable to judge the quality of care provided, base their choices on comfort and appearance. Unfortunately not all make a comparable effort to insure quality of care, which is a function of the quality, experience and training of the staff and of the quality of the programs offered. Of course programs are only as good as the people who run them

While there are many facilities that provide exemplary care and service, there are many others that contribute to the ongoing perception that abuses and neglect of patients are commonplace. With the exception of those facilities where the population is predominantly private pay, many LTC facilities have significant proportions of residents on Medicaid. While funding rules under Medicaid vary from state to state, one would find it difficult to find an administrator who would profess that Medicaid rates are fair and adequate. The result is that LTC administrators are challenged to make the dollars stretch and every scarce dollar spent on aesthetics, marketing and advertising is a dollar not spent on wages, salaries, training and programming. Finding the equilibrium between funds allocated to attracting residents and maintaining an acceptable occupancy rate and also providing quality care is difficult if not impossible. Most facilities simply lack the necessary resources to perform in all facets of their operation.

Quality staffing is by far the biggest challenge and many facilities are a revolving door when assessing the length of service of professional and other direct-care staff. Pay is usually low and benefit packages are typically thin, in some cases non-existent. Working conditions may or may not be good and, as is the case with facilities of any kind that operate twenty-four hours a day, 365 days a year, employees are required to work evening, late night and both weekend and holiday shifts while providing care that is emotionally demanding. Yet, it is the staff more than anything else that determines quality of care.

Facilities that have a director of nursing with solid credentials and broad-based experience are fortunate and experience is often lacking in many other direct care positions. The problem is simple. Nursing homes are challenged to compete with hospitals, medical practices or home health agencies for these professionals.

Long term care is a complicated issue but it can be rolled successfully under the NHCP because of two things. The first is the central mission of the NHCP, which is to provide comprehensive care to all Americans, a mission that does not exclude Americans in nursing homes and other long-term care facilities. The second is that a methodology is already in place to identify when an individual crosses the bridge between those who are able to pay for their care and those who are not.

We propose that the transition of LTC to the National Health Care Plan begin with a delineation of the components of LTC that are health care and those that are related to room and board. Once defined the health care portion of LTC costs would be immediately covered by the NHCP and would be the responsibility of the individual's primary care physician. As with all other patients the primary care physician will be capped for this segment of the population, although at a significantly higher rate. It is imperative that, through the actuarial process, these cap rates are adequate to make these patients attractive to PCPs. Recall again our admonition that our objective is not to squeeze the physician dry, but rather to insure that they have the resources necessary to care for these men and women and still be financially successful.

The component of LTC that is "room and board" related would remain the financial responsibility of the LTC residents and their families, much as is the case today for all LTC costs. When the resident arrives at that threshold necessary to qualify for Medicaid under the current system of care they would, similarly, qualify for full coverage under the NHCP and the PCP's capitation rate would be adjusted appropriately. Recall that the public already pays for this Medicaid coverage, but inefficiently. The Medicaid process is complicated both in terms of meeting the certification requirements for LTC facilities and then collecting payment. All of this complexity will vanish under the NHCP.

It is anticipated that, as a patient reaches the point that long-term care is necessary, the PCP and the patient's family will work together to make the decision to utilize long-term care and to select an appropriate facility. The patient's family wants a facility where they believe their loved one will be comfortable and where they will receive quality care. They want it to be attractive, clean and convenient for them to visit.

The Primary Care Physician has similar interests. Even though, initially, the PCP will not be responsible for the room and board component of the cost they are responsible for the medical care and will want to be satisfied that a facility rises to a standard with which they are comfortable. Working together the family and the PCP will not only make a good decision but will also be placing consumer pressure on the facility.

In order to be the facility of choice the entity must satisfy both customers and they must do so at a competitive price. Under the NHCP pricing will be market driven. If a facility fails to perform in terms of cleanliness and aesthetics either the family or the PCP will become dissatisfied, as both are qualified to judge the facility on these criteria. The facility must also satisfy the physician on the basis of the quality of care. Failure to earn this customer's satisfaction will lead to the decision to move the resident to a more acceptable solution and to the subsequent loss of revenue for the facility. It will also significantly reduce the probability that the PCP will consider the facility in the future and will result in a sullied reputation within the community. The end result will be not only the loss of short-term revenue, but also future sources of revenues.

As with other aspects of the NHCP the shared responsibility between family, patient and physician can only improve the quality of care and it will deepen the loyalty the family is likely to feel for their

PCP. As in all aspects of care under the NHCP, the primary care physician will be incented to keep their patient-families satisfied.

There may be some PCPs who will elect not to retain a patient who enters long term care, not because the financial incentives are inadequate, but because it is not the type of medicine they wish to practice. Similarly there will be other PCPs for whom LTC patient care is enjoyable. The referring PCP will want to be sure the family is happy with the new PCP and the new PCP will want to insure that their colleague is satisfied as this is the best way to maintain a steady stream of referrals.

In this environment not all LTC organizations will survive. Those unable to perform will gradually see their occupancy rates decline until they are forced to close their doors. Those facilities that are able to perform and, as they say in business, meet or exceed the expectations of their customers, will develop a waiting list. These facilities will also, if they wish to enjoy their success for the long-term, continue making new investments in staff and training as well as new capital investments. The capital investments of the more successful facilities will often be focused on increased capacity to meet the growing demand for their service.

Primary care physicians who find the proportion of LTC patients increasing may well employ a registered nurse or nurse practitioner to maintain daily contact with their patients and with the professional staff of the LTC facilities to which they admit.

Physician ownership of LTC facilities has been a source of controversy in the past but we contend the reasons were not that physician ownership is a problem, but that the logic of the current system is defective. Under the NHCP there need be no such controversy as, once again, the interests of the physician and his patients are parallel. Ownership, particularly on the part of physicians who care for a significant number of LTC patients can only give the physician more immediate control over the quality of care.

The optimal situation is one in which the patient's health is maintained, or pain and suffering reduced, for as long as the patient/resident lives and the optimal use of resources is one where this can be done without the need to purchase care outside the LTC facility.

Prescription Drugs and the Drug Industry

Prescription drugs play a major role in the rising cost of health care in the United States. Because Medicare does not cover prescription drugs the issue has become the center of much attention and debate in the political sphere, particularly by such advocacy groups as the AARP. The prescription drug industry is big business. Drug companies in the U.S. and around the world spend billions of dollars on research and development, working under pressure to be the first company to offer exciting new medicines for sale to the public. Whether Prozac, Viagra, or any of a number of other "wonder drugs," ownership of one of the hottest drugs on the market can assure the financial success of the company for several years.

The drug companies also spend millions of dollars on advertising in virtually all media aimed at the general public. Additionally, companies market directly to physicians through a professional sales force armed with a valise full of samples, free dinners, and other inducements. The efforts and dollars are spent, all for one purpose, to influence physicians to prescribe "our" products, not the other guy's.

Retail drug companies, whether national chains such as Walgreen's, CVS and others, invest millions in building convenient new stores to keep the customers coming back. Companies such as Wal-Mart have entered the competition in both in-store pharmacies and "prescription-by-mail," initiatives, the latter a service favored by managed care for the significant savings that accrue.

For the elderly who take multiple prescriptions, the monthly cost can take huge bites out of their monthly Social Security check. We've all heard the horror stories of senior citizens forgoing a portion of their food purchases so they will be able to pay for their medicine.

Of equal concern, although recently lost in the high profile discussion of drug costs, is the problem of people on too many drugs, prescribed by too many physicians, for far too long. In some cases the drugs may not be compatible with one another and in others the duration of the prescriptions may exceed that which is necessary to benefit the patient. The problem is that no one physician has the responsibility of coordinating the treatments given by the primary care doctors and any number of specialists who may not always communicate effectively with one another.

The general practitioner may try to provide such oversight, but often there are simply too many specialists involved with the patient and too much pressure to devote time to revenue generating activity. The pharmacist may also strive to monitor the various drugs prescribed, but often only a portion of the drugs prescribed are filled in a single pharmacy, particularly when the patient's insurance provider has contracted with a mail-in drug service for maintenance drugs.

As with so many other aspects of health care the absence of price as a driving force in the administration of prescription medicine has far-reaching consequences. Not withstanding the many seniors whose drugs are not covered and the millions of others who lack coverage and must pay for whatever drugs they require, many Americans have some level of health coverage that includes a prescription drug benefit. For these individuals cost is the last thing they consider when their physician outlines a treatment plan and the prescriptions he will write. In all probability these individuals, like those who lack any sort of prescription coverage, are unlikely to refuse a prescription because of its cost. So much faith is placed in the judgment of our physicians that we rarely question their decisions.

The physicians themselves do not routinely think about the cost of drugs other than signing that side of the prescription slip that authorizes generic substitution, or offering samples. It is not that they do not care but rather that their attention is so focused on the medical needs of their patients and on collecting payment, that other considerations seem unimportant. In the physician's mind cost is not important to most Americans.

The National Health Care Plan changes almost everything; beginning with the influence that price will play in the physician's prescribing patterns. How will it look?

Research and development of new products will be no less important in the future than it is today and no doubt will require the same investment. Advertising expenditures will require a re-examination, however. It would be naïve to think that advertising is no longer important. Patients do influence their physician's decisions with their requests for specific drugs and physicians are influenced, particularly when given a choice between two comparable products, by the sales representatives with whom they feel the greatest affinity.

Many drug companies will consider significant reductions in dollars budgeted for traditional advertising with some of those dollars reallocated to support of the professional sales force.

The most substantial change in the system will be that price will influence a physician's decisions and contrary to conventional wisdom, this is a good thing, not bad. Today there is no force in the system that can find the optimum level of care, which we would define as the level of care that gives the best value for the dollar. As with the other components of the system, it is in the physician's long-term best interests to provide optimal care for their patients and most Americans would agree that this is also in their best interests. The PCP will take control of the prescription process. They will select drugs that they believe to be the most cost-effective. Instead of prescribing one of two or more similar drugs because of the salesmen, the physician will compare prices. Drugs that are priced above their competitor's product will see sales drop until they are attractively priced. This type of market pressure will have more impact on pricing than a dozen regulations. Drug companies must make a profit, but to do so they must focus on meeting the needs and expectations of their customer.

When acceptable generic substitutes are available the physician will be much more likely to pass on the brand name equivalent and this also will place pressure on the manufacturers and retailers alike to keep pricing in line.

Physicians will also pay close attention to the drugs that are prescribed for a given patient by the specialists with whom the PCP contracts. They will bring all providers together to insure that drugs are compatible. Finally, they will periodically review whether or not it is appropriate to continue a medication for the long term. All of these activities can only serve to improve the quality of care provided to the American people.

Most importantly, under the NHCP, every single American will be able to get the drugs they require. The impact on the poor and the elderly will be most dramatic.

Other Professional Providers

Chiropractors and podiatrists are examples of other providers of professional care who's world will change. Because the services provided by these men and women, particularly chiropractors, are often not covered by insurance it would appear on the surface that their professional life would change only a little. Patients that elect to pay for this care under the current system will likely continue to do so under the NHCP.

In the case of the podiatrist, some do receive referrals from both medical doctors and osteopaths. Whether or not the care provided as a result of these referrals is covered by insurance is not so important as the evidence offered by the referral itself that the podiatrist's services are valued. Whether a PCP will be willing to purchase such services under the NHCP is difficult to predict. The primary care physician will look for ways to relieve the pain and suffering of their patients and should they determine that this or any care contributes to the health and welfare of their patient, the wise physician will certainly consider purchasing this care.

Although referrals from physicians to chiropractors may be less common one would expect the same logic to rule. The only question a responsible primary care physician will ask is whether or not the service produces value for his or her patient.

Other Institutional Providers

Examples of other institutional providers would be the United States Military, the Public Health Service, and private providers who contract with institutions such as prisons to provide care to the institution's residents or inmates.

The U.S. Military

All branches of the U.S. Military have a health component to provide care to military personnel and their dependents. As these health care systems are well established and military personnel move from one military installation to another with some frequency, it may not make sense to tinker with the basic structure of this component of the American health care system.

What could and should change, however, is the manner in which the military health system is funded. Ideally it should be funded in the same way that the balance of the U.S. health care system is funded. Tax dollars should funnel through the National Health Care Plan Fund and should be paid to providers through the same capitation system that serves the balance of the population. In the case of the military, however, the service branch would be recognized as a primary care provider and would be the recipient of the monthly capitation payments for military personnel. Military dependents would be free to choose the military as their "primary care provider" or, alternatively, to select a private provider in the community where they live.

Upon receipt of the capitation payment for military personnel and however many dependents that elect to enroll, the military health organization would then be free to provide comprehensive care in whatever manner they think best. Care could be provided through military facilities and hospitals using military physicians and specialists or, could be purchased from private medical sources in the community where the base or installation is located. In small bases the latter might be a more prudent and economical approach while in large bases with adequate existing facilities the more effective choice might be to use those resources.

What is vital is that the capitation revenue be placed in a dedicated fund within the military organizational structure to insure that those funds are not diverted for other purposes.

In communities where it does not make good fiscal sense to maintain military hospitals and clinics these might well be privatized, allowing the local medical community to provide total care.

Pubic Health Service

In communities currently served by the U.S. Public Health Service, the patients who are the recipients of care should make the decisions. The United States Government could elect to be a "primary care provider" or the system could be privatized. In either case the provider must compete for patients like any other private provider. If the care provided by these entities in any given community is not satisfactory, the patients must be free to choose other providers. As with any community that is under-served or that is dissatisfied with the quality of available care, it should not be too difficult to attract other primary care providers who, upon relocation, would find a ready patient population and the revenue flow that is attached.

Private Institutional Providers

There are a number of companies that contract to provide health care to prisons and other institutional populations. Today these entities are paid per a negotiated contractual arrangement. Under the NHCP we would propose that contracts still be awarded by the institution, but the funding will come through the NHCP as with any other patient population. Undoubtedly during the actuarial process these special populations may be treated differently than patients in the general population.

Insurers, MCOs, Third-party Administrators and Fiscal Intermediaries

Under the NHCP the functions now performed by insurers, managed care companies, third-party administrators and fiscal intermediaries will no longer be required. Those business entities and governmental agencies totally dedicated to health care can be shut down. Corporations competing in other markets, unrelated to health care can re-direct those resources to other markets or eliminate those costs altogether.

Like other industries that have lost products and services to "legislated obsolescence" there will be large numbers of displaced employees. As difficult as this may be for the employees who have lost their jobs, and as politically unpleasant to the politicians and corporate leaders, there are many precedents. Whether industries relocated south of the border as a result of the NAFTA or those shut down when a federal contract is lost, never have we let lost jobs stand in the way of progress. Jobs lost in the aftermath of the NHCP should be treated no differently. It boils down to a choice between extending care to 45 million Americans or protecting the jobs of thousands. The thousands will find other jobs but history and experience tell the story about the likelihood that the 45 millions will find health care.

In general the employees of these peripheral institutions are skilled and well educated and will be relatively easy to re-train and re-employ. We would propose that the government provide assistance to those individuals willing to take advantage of retraining programs, services and resources.

The Issue of Quality Control

The industrial community has made great strides over the last two decades in improving the quality of the products they manufacture or assemble. At the risk of oversimplifying, the improvements are largely the result of the movement away from end-line inspection to implementation of formal quality systems, such as ISO and QS 9000 or Six Sigma, that build quality into the manufacturing or assembly process. This quality model is useful in understanding the logical framework of this new health care system. For years insurance companies, managed care organizations and such government agencies as the Health Care Finance Administration have tried to control the quality of medical decision-making after the fact, with limited medical knowledge, no first-hand familiarity with the patient, and from a distance. Under the NHCP we build controls into the process by giving the payer/customer real power to act on their satisfaction or lack thereof. However insulated they might think they are, providers cannot consistently provide substandard care without losing a customer. Just as importantly, the incentives of the system reward the provider for effective decision-making. As with any endeavor it is always best to do it correctly the first time. The NHCP simply acknowledges that the physician is already the decision-maker and strives to provide incentives for quality and to inject accountability into the process.

Workers Compensation

Work place injuries present some special challenges in the world of the National Health Care Plan. Since all Americans are entitled to free, comprehensive care one might ask why we would need a Workers Comp program? Why, for example, can't an injured worker seek care from his PCP just as he would for any other illness or injury?

One of the problems relates to the primary care physician's financial responsibility for this care. The PCPs will not want to bear sole financial responsibility for treatment of an injury that may have been caused by negligence, inadequate safety guidelines, substandard training, or by the careless act of a co-worker unless those events are taken into consideration during the actuarial process in which capitation rates are established.

Today the legal departments of insurance or managed care companies handle disputes about coordination of benefits and the level of an employer's responsibility. It would not be practical to expect individual primary care physicians to do the same.

Another problem is that employers of injured workers prefer a physician who is neutral and therefore unlikely to give the employee's interests greater consideration than their own. The employer wants the employee to return to work as soon as they are able and also wants some objective assessment as to the legitimacy of the injury and its severity.

It may well be that the best solution is for the employer to continue to purchase workers comp coverage, hence workplace injuries would be treated outside the borders of the NHCP. While this would serve the interests of the employer it may or may not serve the interests of the employee/patient and the PCP. An example would be an injury in which one course of treatment is quick and easy but may have long-term ramifications for the patient's health. The PCP would prefer a treatment plan that considers the total health of the patient in the near and long term. Since a perfect solution is not possible we offer one that should assure quality health care while avoiding unnecessary cost.

Assuming work injuries were considered during the actuarial process, the primary care physician has received some compensation for this care but this does not satisfy the PCP's concern that the employer share the cost. What we propose is an option in which the employee's primary care physician is financially responsible for all care that can be provided within his practice and the employer will be billed for a portion, we recommend eighty percent, of any external services, whether specialty, diagnostic or institutional.

This places much of the burden for serious injuries on the employer yet it is in the interests of the PCP who subcontracted care to be prudent as they also share in its cost. Such an approach would also seem to address the legitimacy issue as the PCP will not be interested in providing or purchasing care for an injury that is exaggerated or fabricated.

Regarding the issue of return to work, whenever an employer questions the appropriateness of such determinations by the employee's personal physician, that employer would be free, at their own expense, to seek a second opinion.

It would seem advisable for most employers to purchase some form of re-insurance to limit their exposure for extraordinary expenses.

Conclusion

Health care is a complicated business and it is not possible to address every aspect of the system that may be impacted by the NHCP. As we noted in Chapter 1, we are not seeking a perfect system, as perfection is unattainable. There will be problems under the NHCP, including many that could not be anticipated. It is our belief that the system can accommodate these issues and find satisfactory solutions. We must also recall that the system we intend to replace is about as far from perfect as a system can be. It is this author's contention that the problems of the existing system are untenable and that the problems to be confronted after implementation of this National Health Care Plan will pale in comparison.

An examination of the British system offers a few clues to what we might expect in the National Health Care Plan. At the beginning of Nineteen Nineties the British introduced a program they referred to as GP Fundholding. In this plan large primary care groups were given the opportunity to volunteer to participate. The Government offered fundholders a "fixed budget (hence fundholding) for primary care of the patients on their rolls. The fixed funds were intended to cover the primary health care plus pharmacy costs and a limited number of specified secondary procedures"(Maddox, 1999). The intent was to create "internal markets featuring contractual relationships between providers" that, ultimately, would improve the quality of primary care in an environment in which there were incentives to be cost-effective. In 1997 the fundholding experiment was replaced by Primary Care Groups, which were mandatory and universal.

While these programs bear similarity to the NHCP proposed herein, it is, as one might suspect in a British program, much more guided by the government and much more structured. There have been positive results that would, however, be objectives in the NHCP. The focus on public health and prevention, collaboration with other health professionals and, continuing education focused on improving the quality of care are examples. In the British system these objectives are directed by the system and there is an attempt to standardize care. In the NHCP we would prefer that providers choose to innovate rather than being directed to do so and although the need to improve quality of care in the U.S. is great, imposing standardized care discourages imagination and innovation. It has been the American tradition that innovation is driven by the market rather than by socialized structure.

The National Health Care Plan fully embraces the market as something good and eschews the socialized approach. We can, however, learn much from the British experience.

"The most important thing people can do for the future of the world is realize that what they do matters."

Jane Goodall

CHAPTER 11
POWER OF THE MASSES

Along with the quote from the remarkable Jane Goodall there are two other thoughts the reader should take with them at the conclusion of their reading. The first is that not only does what individual men and women do matter, but each one of us is a member of one of the most powerful forces on the planet. Each of us is an American consumer. The second thought was one of the ground rules stipulated in the first chapter: Anything man can imagine, man can do.

Not only can you make a difference in the campaign to implement the National Health Care Plan; it cannot happen without you. How many readers have purchased, for their child or a grandchild, a Cabbage Patch Doll, Beanie Baby, Pokemon Cards, or more recently, a volume from the Harry Potter series. Each of you who have made such a purchase contributed to the incredible success these products have enjoyed, just as each voter in the most recent Presidential Election affected the outcome. We each are free to exercise our will to act and we never know when our action will have enormous, far-reaching consequences.

The commitment of each reader is vital to this effort, as only American citizens can bring something of the scope of the National Health Care Plan into being. The President of the United States cannot and neither can your Senators or Representatives. As powerful as these men and women may be, they are, in a very real sense, a prisoner of their positions. These leaders are under tremendous political pressure to accede to the wishes of their party and to the wishes of the political action committees that lobby for their support and which contribute significantly to their campaigns (Weiss, 1997). The pressure to compromise is also a powerful tradition that restricts the freedom of elected representatives at any level of government.

As much as these officials may want to support an idea they need the assurance that it has the support of the voters in their state or congressional district. How we provide such assurance is the subject of this final chapter.

As we have noted the American consumer is one of the most powerful forces in the world and it is this force into which we must tap if we expect to see this health care plan implemented.

It is no easy task to rally the masses on demand – the populace just doesn't respond well to direction. Once rallied, however, the masses have the power to change any aspect of our socio-economic world. Our task is imposing, but not as much as you might think. All we want to do is change the way we preserve the health of our people and the way we pay for that activity. To do this requires sweeping legislation. Such legislation is not difficult to pass if we can gain the support of our congressional representatives and senators, and these men and women can be swayed if a significant proportion of their constituency show support.

Typically when the masses are rallied, it is not as a result of some direction given by our government, but rather the response of large numbers of people to an idea; an idea that fires the imagination. This is the point at which we begin. We hope this new idea about the way we deliver health care in the United States will strike the fancy of the masses and that people will respond much as they do when introduced to an exciting new consumer product. In the case of consumer products, the process is simple. We rush to wherever it is that the product or service is sold and we make a purchase. We need nobody's permission, we need no one to show us how.

The power of the consumer can change an entire industry just by switching from one product to another. The recording industry provides a perfect example. No one legislated the obsolescence of the phonograph record; the industry simply offered a new alternative and the public rather quickly made the switch to tape cassettes. Today the compact disc is replacing the cassette tape. Such changes are simply a function of providing consumers with a new choice in an environment where they have the freedom to act. The consumer isn't even conscious of this power.

Cabbage Patch dolls, Beanie Babies, Pokemon Cards and Harry Potter provide other examples. The public could have just as easily ignored these products and carried some other product to market dominance. Did the makers of these products have a marketing plan? Of course they did, but every marketing executive will tell you there is no sure method of predicting or influencing the consumer public. One must simply offer an attractive product that catches the consumer's imagination and communicate the product's benefits and availability. The rest is up to individual consumers. If a sufficient number like the product and choose to make a purchase, the world changes.

Our objective is to tap this same power of the consumer, but even if we are successful in creating the excitement it may not be obvious what action people can take to demonstrate their support. Think of how it might work.

A new health care system is proposed in a book entitled *Radical Surgery: Reconstructing the American Health Care System*. The work itself must be of sufficient quality to catch the imagination of the public and the author and publisher must bring it to the attention of a sufficient number of readers. If enough readers respond to the book and make a purchase and then tell their friends and family about it, the book will appear on the best-seller list.

If a sufficient number of those readers take the action we will shortly recommend, and encourage their friends and family to do so, then something quite magical will happen.

As the author I have done my best to offer an innovative idea that would solve the American health care crisis. Along with my publisher I have done the best I can to market the book to bring it to the attention of you, the reader. The rest is entirely up to you.

My request of each reader, assuming you see value in the health plan I have presented, is that you take action. It will cost you very little and will inconvenience you only slightly, but if you act it can change the world of health care in America.

What you are asked to do is simple.

Begin by copying the sample letter at the end of this chapter. Make five copies of it each month; address and sign it and include your voter's registration number, and then mail copies to:

Your Congressional Representative
Both of your state's United States Senators
The Governor of your state, and
The President of the United States.

Mail the letter to your Congressional Representative and Senators to their Washington offices, as this will magnify the effect as letters begin to arrive.

The next step is to repeat this process each month until the National Health Care Plan, un-compromised, becomes the law of the land.

Thirdly, that those of you who are not registered to vote do so and make note of that action in each of the letters you mail.

Finally, that you spread the word. Tell your friends, your family, your neighbors and co-workers about it and ask them to do the same. When you make a new acquaintance, tell them about *Radical Surgery* and ask them to read the book. You can loan them your copy, refer them to the library or, make the author and publisher happy by suggesting that they purchase a copy of their own. Ask them to show their own support and join the letter writing campaign.

This is optional, but if you are married or have a significant other, it would double the impact if each of you send a letter rather than sending one as a couple.

In today's age of technology there are many methods that can be used for such communication. Other than a letter one could place a telephone call, send a fax or, send an e-mail. Although any of these options are acceptable it is my recommendation that you send your letter through the mail. A recipient can screen out telephone calls, delete an e-mail, and destroy a fax (besides receipt of thousands of faxes and telephone calls could disrupt the operation of an office and this is not our intent). There is something about a letter or a stack of letters or, better yet, a canvas bag full of letters, that commands the recipient's attention. The beauty of a letter through the mail is that letters have mass. One hundred letters might come to you in a stack with a rubber band. Receive a thousand letters and it is delivered to you in a canvas bag. Receive ten thousand letters and you will have them piled on the floor. Large numbers are impossible to ignore.

It is understood that, in the aftermath of the September 11th attacks and the subsequent incidences of anthrax sent through the mail, the reader may be reluctant to use the U.S. Mail. It would be inappropriate for me to tell you what to do and each of you must make your own decision about the method of communication. What is important is that you just take action.

Imagine the impact on an elected representative, should he or she receive a letter or other communication from one out of every fifty constituents asking for his or her support of the National Health Care Plan presented in *Radical Surgery*. Imagine if he or she received such a letter once a month. Imagine further if the Governor and each Senator in the state received such a letter on a monthly basis. If each representative receives 5000 letters per month and the state has ten congressional districts, the governor and senators would each receive 50,000 letters per month. Based upon the same numbers the President of the United States would receive over 3 million letters each month.

If every reader would maintain diligence in continually expanding the number of citizens who participate, these numbers would increase each and every month.

Are there any of our elected representatives, republican or democrat, male or female, white or of color, young or old who would feel so secure in their office that they could choose to ignore such a groundswell? What if the percentage of supporters grew to 5 percent, or 10 percent, or even more? Go a step further to imagine how these politicians would respond if, following receipt of these letters the number of new registered voters in their district were to increase by a significant proportion.

Is this too much to ask of American citizens concerned about health care and wanting to do something about it? It doesn't seem like much at all. The cost of taking this action for a period of twenty months would cost each reader:

A box of 100 envelopes	$2.50
100 sheets of printer paper	$1.00
100 first class postage stamps	$34.00

For a total of $37.50 or less than two dollars per month we can change the world.

Think how much more effort it took for us to propel Beanie Babies to an unprecedented level of consumer popularity. Understand that we were not conscious of our role in the elevation of Beanie Babies to such heights, we were just acting in response to our material wants by making a purchase. No one had to tell us what to do, but it did require some degree of effort. We had to learn where Beanie Babies were being sold; we had to get there before the supply was exhausted, sometimes fighting through crowds of people on the same mission, and then we had to wait in line. We also had to pay cash money for our Beanie Baby and for some of us finding the cash was in itself a hardship. We did what we had to do, however, as if our quality of life would some how deteriorate if we didn't get that

Beanie Baby – or more often, if we didn't get just one more Beanie Baby.

It was just a few of us here and there who made it happen, but added together across the whole nation it was millions of people acting to achieve the same end. Striving for the same end but acting independently. Occasionally we would call our friends and relatives and let them in on the action. No one purchase was any more or less important than the others and none of them would have been important without the others. All rivers begin with a trickle, even the great ones.

If we would go to all this trouble to buy a Beanie Baby, wouldn't we make a similar effort to change our health care system? All the power we need is at our disposal. It is a matter of exercising our will.

Whatever you do, don't forget to vote on Election Day. Imagine the impact if, after being besieged by these communications our elected officials see the voter turnout increased by a significant percent.

If you are reading this it is vital that you do your part. The power of the special interest groups can be overcome only by the power of the masses. The health insurance and managed care industries can be a powerful force and they will have little choice but to fight this or any other national health care plan – their very existence is at stake.

It's hard to predict where the American Medical Association will stand, but they might well perceive this proposal as a threat. All change is difficult and radical change is exponentially more difficult to handle. If physicians take the time to study and to understand this proposal, however, they may realize the advantages of a health care system in which they are in control. The advantages of managing cash flow rather than receivables may also catch their eye and one would think that an environment without insurance companies and managed care organizations would be appealing.

Imagine the impact if one quarter of all primary care physicians would flex their aggregate political muscle and provide information about the proposed National Health Care Plan to their patients and encourage them to join the letter writing campaign.

The position of the American Hospital Association would be no easier to predict. No doubt the revolutionary changes would be frightening to leaders in this industry. If they would also take the time to understand the NHCP they might begin to envision advantages.

Doing business and negotiating with local physicians, many of whom have long-standing affiliation with the hospital might seem more appealing than dealing with a complicated array of insurance carriers, HMOs and PPOs, not to mention the Health Care Finance Administration.

Imagine the impact if the AHA would publicly support the NHCP proposal and if hospitals were to encourage their employees and patients to join the letter writing campaign.

And what about employers across the land? The National Health Care Plan would eliminate their need to be concerned about health care. No more concerns about health benefits and no more decisions about which carrier to choose and no more of the hassle of open enrollment periods and all of the other details involved in providing a health care benefit. Imagine if even a quarter of American employers would encourage their employees to join the letter writing campaign.

Whatever your prediction about the impact of these channels of support, any one of these groups could bring significant pressure to bear and if all would act the impact would be phenomenal.

There are millions of Americans who are too poor and disenfranchised to hear this clarion call. They may be too ill; they may be too old or too frail. They may sleep in a homeless shelter and eat in a soup kitchen. They may be found in many places, but is there any doubt in your mind that these Americans would favor a program that assures them of quality medical care while sparing them the indignity of a free clinic or Medicaid.

These people are counting on you and so are we.

APPENDIX A

The Honorable_____
United States House of Representatives
Washington, DC 20515

Dear Representative _____:

The American Health Care System is at a point of crisis in which 45 million Americans lack health care or coverage and millions more worry that they may lose coverage if they were to lose their job.

This problem must be resolved and I am asking for your support for the proposal for a National Health Care Plan developed by Mel Hawkins and detailed in his book, *Radical Surgery: Reconstructing the American Health Care System.* This health care proposal offers an innovative solution that will:

- provide comprehensive care and prescription drugs to all American citizens,
- give the patient free choice of physician,
- enable doctors to practice quality medicine without interference of public or private bureaucrats,
- reduce aggregate health care expenditures by as much as $200 billion per year,
- rely on free market forces to ensure quality, internal to the process, obviating the need for the health insurance and managed care industries, and
- eliminate Medicare and Medicaid and limit the role of government to the few things governments do well.

I am a registered voter and will cast my vote only for candidates who declare their support for this vital proposal in its entirety, without compromise.

Thank you in advance for your support.

Sincerely,   Voter's Registration No.:

APPENDIX B

The other letters would be addressed to:

The Honorable_____
United States Senate
Washington, DC 20510

Dear Senator _____:

The Honorable_____
Governor of the State of _____
_____

Dear Governor _____:

The Honorable_____
President of the United States
The White House
Washington, DC 20500

Dear Mr. President:

BIBLIOGRAPHY

Anderson Consulting: Ken Jennings, Ph.D., Kurt Miller, Sharyn Materna. *Changing Health Care: Creating Tomorrow's Winning Health Enterprise Today.* Knowledge Exchange, Santa Monica, CA, 1997.

Armstrong, Pat and Hugh with Claudia Fegan, MD, *Universal Healthcare: What the United States Can Learn from the Canadian Experience.* The New York Press, New York, 1998.

Bindman, Andrew B., Jonathon P. Weiner, and Azeem Majeed, "Primary Care Groups in the United Kingdom: Quality and Accountability," *Health Affairs*, 20:3, (May-June 2001): 132-145.

Budrys, Grace, *Our Unsystematic Health Care System*, Rowman & Littlefield Publishing, Landham, MD, 2001.

Covey, Stephen R., The *7 Habits of Highly Effective People: Powerful Lessons in Personal Change*, A Fireside Book, Simon & Schuster, New York, 1989.

Drache, Daniel, Editor et al, *Market Limits in Health Reform: Public Success, Private Failure*, Routledge, London/New York,1999.

Dranove, David, *The Economic Evolution of American Health Care*, Princeton Univ Press, Princeton, NJ, 2000.

Eck, MD, Aleita, "Funding Health Care through the Church," *The Changing Face of Health Care: A Christian Appraisal of Managed Care, Resource Allocation, and Patient-Caregiver Relationships*, edited by John F. Kilner, Robert D. Orr and Judith Allen Shelly, William B. Eerdmans Publishing Company, Grand Rapids, MI, 1998.

Epstein, Richard A., *Mortal Peril: Our Inalienable Right to Health Care?*, Perseus Press, Cambridge, MA, 2000.

Friend, MD, David B., *Healthcare.com Rx for Reform*, CRC Press – St. Lucie Press, Boca Raton, FL, 2000.

Glied, Sherry, *Chronic Condition: Why Health Reform Fails*, Harvard Univ. Press, Cambridge, Mass., 1998.

Gollatz, John W., *Society's Mirror: Reflections on Health Care Reform*, Health Information Press, Los Angeles, 1998.

Goodman, John C. and Gerald L. Musgrave, *Patient Power: The Free-Enterprise Alternative to the Clinton Health Plan* (Abridged), Cato Inst., Washington, D.C., 1994.

Gornick, Marian E., *Vulnerable Populations and Medicare Services: Why Do Disparaties Exist*, Century Foundation Press, New York, 2000.

Grumbach, K., Joe V. Selby, Cheryl Damberg, Andrew B. Bindman, Charles Quesenberry, Jr., Alison Truman and Connie Uratsu, "Resolving the Gatekeeper Conundrum: What Patients Value in Primary Care and Referrals to Specialists," *Journal of the American Medical Association*, Jul 21, 1999, p. 261-66.

Heirich, Max, *Rethinking Health Care: Innovation and Change in America*, Westview Press, Boulder, Co., 1998.

Helms, Robert B. and Robert Helms, Editors, *Medicare in the 21st Century: Seeking Fair and Efficient Reform*, AEI Press, Washington, DC, 1999.

Herzlinger, Regina E., *Consumer-Driven Health Care: Implications for Providers, Players and Policy-Makers*, Jossey-Bass, San Francisco, 2001.

Himmelstein, David U. and Steffie Woodhandler, with Ida Hellander, *Bleeding the Patient: The Consequences of Corporate Healthcare*, Common Courage Press, Monroe, ME, 2001.

Institute of Medicine, Editor, *Crossing the Quality Chasm: A New Health System for the 21st Century*, 2000.

Jacobs, Alan, "Seeing Difference: Market Health Reform in Europe," *Journal of Health Politics, Policy and Law*, 23:1, Feb 1998.

Kilner, John F., Robert D. Orr, and Judith Allen Shelly, Ed., *The Changing Face of Health Care: A Christian Appraisal of Managed Care, Resource Allocation, and Patient Giver Relationships*. William B. Eerdmans Publishing Co., Grand Rapids, MI/Cambridge, UK, 1998.

Kindig, M.D., Ph.D., David A., *Purchasing Population Health: Paying for Results*, The University of Michigan Press, Ann Arbor, 1997.

Klein, Rudolf, "Why Britain is Reorganizing Its National Health Service – Yet Again," *Health Affairs*, 17:4 (July-August 1998): 111-125.

Klienke, J. D., *Bleeding Edge: The Business of Health Care in the New Century*, Aspen Publishers, Gaithersburg, MD, 1998.

Le Grand, Julian, "Competition, Cooperation, Or Control? Tales From the British National Health Service," *Health Affairs*, 18:3 (May-June 1999): 27-39.

Lundberg, George D, MD., *Severed Trust: Why American Medicine Hasn't Been Fixed,*. Basic Books, New York, 2001.

Lutz, Sandy, *Med Inc.: How Consolidation is Shaping Tomorrow's Healthcare System*. Jossey-Bass Publishers. San Francisco. 1998.

Maddox, George L., "General Practice Fundholding in the British National Health Service Reform, 1991-1997: GP Accounts of the Dynamic Changes" *Journal of Health Politics, Policy and Law*, 24:4 Aug 1999.

Makover, Michael E., MD, *Mismanaged Care: How Corporate Medicine Jeopardizes Your Health*, Prometheus Books. Amherst, NY, 1998.

McGuire, Michael T. and William H. Anderson, *The US Healthcare Dilemma: Mirrors and Chains*, Auburn House Publishing, Westport, CT, 1999.

Michael, R.N., M.S., J.D., Janet E., "The Impact of Managed Care on Medical Practice," *The Changing Face of Health Care: A Christian Appraisal of Managed Care, Resource Allocation, and Patient-Caregiver Relationships*, edited by John F. Kilner, Robert D. Orr and Judith Allen Shelly, William B. Eerdmans Publishing Company, Grand Rapids, MI, 1998.

Mechanic, David, "The Functions and Limitations of Trust in the Provision of Medical Care," *The Journal of Health Politics, Policy and Law*, 23(1998): 661-86.

Minoque, Tom with Bob Thaves (Illustrator), *We Did All We Could, but Your Healthcare Died: The Patient's New Role in Vital Reforms*, Wyndham Hall Press, Bristol, IN, 2000.

Morrison, Ian, *Health Care in the New Millennium: Vision, Values and Leadership*, Jossey-Bass, San Francisco, 2000.

National Academy Press, *America's Health Care Safety Net: Intact But Endangered*, Washington, DC, 2000.

National Coalition of Health Care, "The National Coalition on Health Care Consumer Survey," Washington, DC, 1997.

O'Brien, Lawrence J., *Bad Medicine: How the American Medical Establishment is Ruining Our Healthcare System*, Prometheus Books, Amherst, NY, 1999.

Peterson, Mark A., Editor, *Healthy Markets?: The New Competition in Medical Care*, Duke Univ. Press, Durham, NC, 1998.

PriceWaterhouseCoopers, "Patients or Paperwork?: The Regulatory Burden Facing America's Hospitals," Commissioned by the American Hospital Association, Chicago, May 2001.

Raffel, Marshall W. and Camile K. Barsukiewicz, *The US Health System Origins & Functions*, Delmar Publishers, Albany, NY, 2001.

Ranade, Wendy, Editor, *Markets and Health Care: A Comparative Analysis*, Addison-Wesley Longman, New York, 1998.

Scott, Claudia Devita, *Public and Private Roles in Health Care Systems: Experiences From Seven Countries (State of Health)*, Open Univ. Press, Buckingham, 2001.

Senge, Peter, *The Fifth Discipline: The Art & Practice of The Learning Organization*, Doubleday, New York, 1990.

Shi, Leiyu and Douglas A. Singh, *Delivering Health Care in America: A Systems Approach*, 2nd Edition, Aspen Publishers, Gaithersburg, MD, 2001.

Shortell, Stephen M., *Remaking Health Care in America*, Jossey-Bass, San Francisco, 2000.

Sparrow, Malcomb K., *License to Steal: How Fraud Bleeds America's Health Care System*, Westview Press, Boulder, CO, 2000.

F. M. Trevino, E. Moyer, B. Valdez, and C. A. Stroup-Benham, "Health Insurance Coverage and Utilization of Health Services by Mexican Americans, Mainland Puerto Ricans, and Cuban Americans," *JAMA* 265 (1991): 233-37; C. Halton, D. L. Wood, V. Burciaga, M. Pereyra, and N. Duan, "Medicaid Enrollment and Health Services Access by Latino Children in Inner-city Los Angeles," *JAMA* 277 (1997): 636-41.

Ubel, Peter A., *Pricing Life: Why Its Time for Health Care Rationing*. A Bradford Book, the MIT Press, Cambridge, MA, 2000.

Weiss, Lawrence D., *Private Medicine and Public Heatlh: Profits, Politics and Prejudice in the American Health Care Enterprise*. Westview Press, A Division of Harper Collins Publishers. Boulder, Colorado, 1997.

Wong, Kenman L., *Medicine and the Marketplace: The Moral Dimensions of Managed Care*, University of Notre Dame Press, Notre Dame, IN, 2000.

ABOUT THE AUTHOR

A former manager of a multi-specialty medical group practice, Mel Hawkins has also served as a director of a county-owned, 500-bed, long-term care facility, with terms as both President and Chair of the Finance Committee. The author has also served as Court Executive of a unified trial court, Chief Operating Officer of a industrial distribution and inventory management company, principle of a management consulting practice and a small business owner, giving Mr. Hawkins nearly thirty years of leadership experience in both the public and private sectors. This varied leadership experience has given Mr. Hawkins a unique and eclectic perspective, one that has served him well as an innovator and problem solver.

Educated at Manchester College where he received a BA degree in Religion and Philosophy and Peace Studies, the author also earned a Master of Science in Education from Saint Francis College and a Master of Public Affairs from Indiana University.

It was during his tenure as a medical group manager that it became apparent to Mel, that there must be a way to deliver health care to the whole population, without sacrificing the great strengths of the American health care system.

Mel Hawkins resides with his wife in Fort Wayne, Indiana, their three children now grown.

Active in his community, Mr. Hawkins attended Leadership Fort Wayne. In addition to his work on the Board of Managers of Byron Health Center, he has also served on the board of the Martin Luther King Montessori School; as a co-founder and a board member of the Boys and Girls Club of Fort Wayne and, as a co-founder, board member and former president of the South Side Business Group of Fort Wayne and Allen County.

www.ingramcontent.com/pod-product-compliance
Lightning Source LLC
Chambersburg PA
CBHW031630110626
46523CB00055B/323